STUFF CHRISTIANS LIKE

JONATHAN ACUFF

ZONDERVAN®

ZONDERVAN.com/
AUTHORTRACKER
follow your favorite authors

ZONDERVAN

Stuff Christians Like
Copyright © 2010 by Jonathan Acuff

This title is also available as a Zondervan ebook.
Visit www.zondervan.com/ebooks.

This title is also available in a Zondervan audio edition.
Visit www.zondervan.fm.

Requests for information should be addressed to:
Zondervan, *Grand Rapids, Michigan 49530*

Library of Congress Cataloging-in-Publication Data

Acuff, Jonathan M.
　　Stuff Christians like / Jonathan Acuff.
　　　　p. cm.
　　ISBN 978-0-310-31994-8 (softcover)
　　　　1. Christian life — Anecdotes. 2. Wit and humor — Religious aspects — Christianity.
　　I. Title.
　　BV4517.A28　2010
　　270.8'30207 — dc22　　　　　　　　　　　　　　　　　　2009046394

Interior design and illustrations: Mark Sheeres

Printed in the United States of America

10 11 12 13 14 15 16 17 18 • 20 19 18 17 16 15 14 13 12 11 10 9 8 7 6 5 4 3 2 1

Stuff Jon Likes: Jenny.

CONTENTS

INTRODUCTION

If you buy this book, God will make you rich.

I was going to say, "If you *read* this book," but I'm pretty sure people who get it at the library won't receive the same amount of awesomeness as people who buy it.

So if you're standing in the bookstore right now, debating whether to buy this book, I guess the real question is, "Do you like money?"

And a really nice car?

And having a better marriage?

And polite children?

And two well-defined eyebrows?

If you answered yes to any of those questions, I'm not sure why you're still on the fence.

Do you love Jesus? Me too. This book is for you.

Do you think we Christians are weird? Me too. This book is for you.

I guess what I'm trying to say is that this book is for everyone. Everyone who has enough lettuce to support my shoe fetish. I'm kidding; that's a Fergie lyric, not a reflection of my heart. I shouldn't even know she exists, never mind be quoting her song in a book published by the people who also publish the Bible.

To make it even easier to jump into *Stuff Christians Like*, I pulled five essays out to get you started. Take a look at them, but if you're standing in the Christian Inspiration section of the bookstore, please go read this by the magazines. Someone is going to witness to you if you stand by so many Bibles for too long.

RANKING HONEYMOON SEX SLIGHTLY HIGHER THAN THE SECOND COMING OF CHRIST

Christians all over the world like the idea of Jesus coming back again, but only if they've lost their virginity first.

And if that's you, if you're a Christian and you've never been married and had sex, let me first say, congratulations. You, my friend, are a unicorn of purity. Second, let me assure you that your expectations of what your honeymoon night is going to be like are probably pretty dead-on. I know deep down there's a part of you thinking, "I am going to be so mad at Jesus if he comes back before I get to have sex."

That's a fair thought; sex is pretty amazing.

Bear in mind that what you and I are saying is that the return of the Messiah is slightly less awesome than intercourse. (I used the word *Messiah* there just to kick the guilt up a notch or two.) If that's your expectation, if you are heralding your honeymoon night as outshining the return of Jesus in both magnificence and magnitude, I think you're going to be just fine.

Because that's pretty much exactly what it's like.

Chances are, you'll be one of those rare people who doesn't need to grow and nurture a marital sexual relationship over sixty years or so. (Ugh ... I just used the words "sexual relationship" and "sixty years" in the same sentence.) You'll instantly and spontaneously know exactly how to do whatever it is that your husband or wife is all about. You'll know all the right buttons to push and you'll laugh, oh you'll laugh at all those people who couldn't figure out the whole thing on the night of their wedding, one of their most physically, emotionally, and mentally exhausting days ever. Suddenly all those wry Christian jokes about not caring about the destination or the weather because you'll never be leaving the hotel room on your honeymoon will make sense, the sun will probably set in a beautiful kaleidoscope of pinks and oranges, and birds in palm trees will tweet out a Prince song. And two porpoises will continuously leap into the air, forming the shape of a heart, symbolizing two Christians becoming one.

That might happen.

I don't remember things being exactly that way on my own honeymoon.

But that might happen for you.

KEEPING CHRIST IN CHRISTMAS

Christians are very protective of their holidays. Just try to write a Christian a note referring to the Celebration of the Birth of their Savior as "Xmas," and you'll see what I mean. Or talk to their kids about Santa—chances are, by the time they can talk, they know that Santa's not real and that "Jesus is the Reason for the Season."

One year though, someone tried to test that theory by giving my family an "Elf on the Shelf." If you're not familiar with that, it's essentially a small elf doll that comes with a book. The book tells you that you're supposed to hide the elf each night during the holiday season and let your kids find it. It's magic or a messenger of Santa or something. It was wildly popular a few years ago and is probably continuing to sell well.

But as I started to think about the whole "real meaning of Christmas" debate, and the "Is Santa bad?" discussion you're almost required by law to have if you're a Christian, I started to wonder about that elf. He was just sitting there, with a smug look on his face, perched on the fireplace mantel, hovering over our nativity scene on the hearth. Instead of the traditional Santa-vs.-Jesus discussion, I began to imagine what would happen if that elf ever ran into the characters from the nativity scene ...

WISE MAN 1: Whoa, whoa, whoa! Who are *you*?

ELF ON THE SHELF: Hi! I'm Elf on the Shelf.

WISE MAN 1: I can see that. It's right there on your box. But what are you doing here?

ELF ON THE SHELF: I came to spread holiday cheer and tell people about the magic of Santa Claus.

WISE MAN 1: That sentence is wrong on so many levels, I don't even know where to start. First of all, please help me understand what "holiday cheer" is. Is that some sort of glitter? Like pixie dust or giggle spray or other elf razzle dazzle?

WISE MAN 2: Slow down, myrrh man. No need to get sarcastic.

WISE MAN 1: You stay out of this, gold guy, and don't call me myrrh man. It's "M&M." No one even knows what myrrh is. My name sounds like some sort of aquatic creature. I knew I should have brought the gold. Everybody loves you. My gift is judged as slightly better than paprika or cinnamon. Awesome.

WISE MAN 3: Myrrh man, Christmas is not about the gifts we give. It's first and foremost about the gift we received: Jesus Christ.

WISE MAN 1: I know, I know, frankincense fella. It's just that you don't understand the pressure I'm under with the myrrh reputation. At least your gift sounds like Frankenstein and is easy to remember. When people say my gift, they don't even know where to finish the word. They always just kind of trail off and say myrhhhhhhhh with, like, fourteen h's. But this isn't about me. This is about this punk elf.

ELF ON THE SHELF: Hi! I'm Elf on the Shelf.

WISE MAN 1: Here you go again. There's no shelf in the nativity scene and therefore no elf. I've got some good news and some bad news for you. The good news is, I'm wearing my traveling robes and won't be able to tune you up myself. The bad news is, the shepherds are always up for a beat down.

SHEPHERD 1: What's going on?

WISE MAN 1: This Peter Pan–looking doll over here is trying to distract us from the birth of Christ. He's trying to steal some of baby Jesus' thunder.

SHEPHERD 2: Oh, really? Not on *my* watch. It's on like Donkey Kong.

ELF ON THE SHELF: "On like Donkey Kong"? That sounds violent. Can't we all just giggle and watch my delightful movie *Elf*, starring Hollywood's Will Ferrell and that rapscallion James Caan?

SHEPHERD 3: People overestimate how clean and well-behaved we shepherds were back in the day. We were like longshoremen. Think of us less as care-takers of sheep and more as pastoral hooligans. We live under the stars and wrestle bears for fun. David was a shepherd and he cut Goliath's head off.

ELF ON THE SHELF: (Gulp.)

SHEPHERD 1: Don't worry. We're not going to do that to you. We *are* going to bounce you out of town like a super ball, though. Drummer boy, cue my theme song.

ELF ON THE SHELF: Wait! The drummer boy wasn't at the birth of Christ either. Why isn't he getting the bum rush?

SHEPHERD 1: Because Jesus is funky and loves a good beat. Plus, every superhero needs a theme song.

WISE MAN 1: You're a superhero now? When did *that* happen? I must have missed that in the Bible.

SHEPHERD 1: Easy Myrrh-lin, wizard of questionable gifts. According to the book of Matthew, you guys didn't even make it to the manger. And at least you have a name. I'm just lumped in as a "shepherd." I have no identity. I had to create my own—hence the theme song.

WISE MAN 1: Good grief!

ELF ON THE SHELF: That's from *Charlie Brown's Christmas*!

SHEPHERD 1: You're still here? Let's do this thing.

(Elf beat down commences.)

BOOTY, GOD, BOOTY

The archives don't go back far enough, but I think that this is exactly the kind of idea that Billy Graham launched his ministry with when he was coming up. It makes sense too because Christians really like "Booty, God, Booty."

I realized this while listening to my favorite radio station in Atlanta, V103, "The People's Station." It's a hip-hop station that plays mostly rap and R&B. The best thing about V103 is their morning show. Every day at 6:30 a.m. when I'm driving to work, they have a segment called the "Inspirational Vitamin." They read a Bible verse and play a gospel song or a clip by a minister from Atlanta. I honestly find it to be an uplifting experience overall. The thing I find most interesting, however, is how they wedge the Inspirational Vitamin into their normal programming.

What often happens is that at 6:25 a.m., right before they transition to the spiritual segment of the show, they play some sort of booty song. Let's say, "I'm 'n Luv (Wit a Stripper)." Then they do the Bible verse at 6:30 a.m. And then they go right back to something like Lil' Wayne "Lollipop" at 6:35 a.m. They essentially bookend the Inspirational Vitamin with booty, following a fairly simple formula: Booty, God, Booty.

It's easy to laugh at how insincere that Inspirational Vitamin seems when it's sandwiched between hardcore rap songs, but maybe God is listening to the broadcast of my day, and this is what he hears:

Saturday night, out on the town. God's at home babysitting my stuff.

Sunday morning, back with God. We're tight. We're praying. We're BFF.

Monday, back at work. God's in the car, where I left my Bible.

It might not be as graphic or as neon, but the juxtaposition between who I am when I'm in "God mode" and who I am when I'm not is pretty substantial. Next time you transition between two parts of your day, ask yourself, "Did I just Booty, God, Booty?"

That's my inspirational vitamin for today.

USING "FAITH LIKE A CHILD" AS AN ESCAPE POD FROM DIFFICULT THEOLOGICAL DISCUSSIONS

I want to be honest with you. If we ever meet and you corner me with a really difficult theological discussion that involves the word *hermeneutics* or *tri-millennialism* or what exactly is going to happen during the end-times, I'm going to climb into my "faith like a child" escape pod and blast away from the conversation.

FRIEND: Jon, do you think the earth was created in six literal days or do days mean something different in God's sense of time?

ME: Hmm, faith like a child.

FRIEND: Sure, sure, childlike faith, that's great, but have you ever thought about the limits of God? He can't lie, so does that mean he's not all-powerful? Because he doesn't possess the ability to lie?

ME: That's a great question. I'm going to go with ... "faith like a child."

FRIEND: Right, but I think God gave us this wonderful mind to explore the deepest truths. Plus, the Bible says we're supposed to put away childish things.

ME: AFLAC.

FRIEND: The insurance company with that annoying duck? What does that have to do with anything?

ME: A Faith like a Child. AFLAC.

FRIEND: That is horrible. You should be ashamed of yourself.

ME: You don't have to be funny if you've got childlike faith. Name one funny five-year-old you've ever met. One told me a knock knock joke the other day that ended with, "Who's there? A tornado broke Cinderella's hair."

FRIEND: Why do we hang out?

ME: Because if I become a famous Christian, I'll take you as my guest to the Dove Awards.

Ninety percent of my conversations with friends end with those two lines.

Is that a bad thing? Do you disagree? What's that you're saying? You've got four different Hebrew phrases that challenge my childlike faith belief? It's hard to hear you through this escape pod door. I'm sorry, you're breaking up. Blast off!

BEING NOT FUNNY FOR THE LORD

Christians don't like being funny. If I had a dollar for every time someone told me, "My favorite thing about Christians is that they're so funny," I would have to dance in the street for nickels to pay my bills. An abundance of humor or wit or satire is rarely a label Christians have been saddled with as a culture.

At first I thought maybe it was God's fault, that perhaps in the Old Testament he dropped an elbow of justice on the Israelites or Amalekites or some other "ites" about their joking ways. But the more I read the Bible, the more I realized that God is pro laughter. My favorite example is Psalm 126: 1–3: "When the Lord brought back the captives to Zion, we were like men who dreamed. Our mouths were filled with laughter, which we spat out as fast as we could because Christians aren't supposed to laugh." I'm kidding. The verse ends with, "Our mouths were filled with laughter, our tongues with songs of joy. Then it was said among the nations, 'The Lord has done great things for them.'"

The nations saw how good God was because of how much his people were laughing. Wow, that is awesome. So how did we get such a bad reputation of being serious people? I blame Somber Christian Syndrome.

Somber Christian Syndrome (SCS) is a disease that tells you that to be considered a good Christian, you have to be serious all the time. That to really reach people for God's kingdom, you have to be holy and reverent, and instead of laughing out loud, you have to quietly remark, "That's funny. I see the humor in that situation. That's funny."

When I started to write *Stuff Christians Like*, I found SCS laced throughout the first chapters. I ended every essay I was writing with a literary call to the altar. Even the goofy ones would start out funny, but then they would eventually work their way around to conclusions that essentially said, "And that's the reason why you have to accept the blood of Jesus Christ into your soul. Ahhhhhhhaleulah." (That's how you spell the way monks sound when they chant. Go ahead and google it. I'll wait.)

In the midst of my bout with SCS, I ran across a verse in Matthew 6. Jesus says in verse 16, "When you fast, do not look somber as the hypocrites do, for they disfigure their faces to show men they are fasting."

He's preaching about people who attempt to look holy, people who disfigure their faces to look more spiritual than other people. Even though that verse is about fasting, I found it very convicting about what I was writing.

Somber Christian Syndrome is all about looking holy, about appearing more spiritual than other people and making everyone think you're perfect. And that's what I was doing with my writing. I was trying to force-feed serious insights into every essay so that someone would read the book and say, "By jove, his blog is funny, but this book is drenched in wisdom and holiness. He very well may be the next C. S. Lewis." Which on a side note, I probably could have been if my publisher hadn't rejected the original title suggestion for this book, *Stuff Christians Like: The book C. S. Lewis would have written if he had been 40 percent more sarcastic and 100 percent less dead.*

What's the cure for SCS? The verses in Matthew suggest putting oil on your head and washing your face. If that doesn't work, put some oil on your face and tell people it's "Sermon Sheen" and that you're pretending to be a sweaty minister. Sweaty minister material always kills.

MY BAD

One time I went to an R-rated movie with a friend who works at a church. On the way out he noticed two people who knew him. He grabbed me before they recognized us and we hid out until we thought they were gone. Turns out they waited for us in the hall. I didn't work at a church, so all I had done was commit a regular sin. My friend had broken some sort of church employee, "Never see the movie *Desperado* starring Latin sensation Antonio Banderas" covenant, so I immediately threw him under the bus and said, "It's embarrassing, really, seeing pastors behave like this. The three of us are all just normal Christians; this guy is a professional. He should be ashamed of himself." Then I swore for emphasis, but it was one of the okay swears, so it wasn't that big of a deal.

COMPLAINING ABOUT NOT BEING "FED" AT CHURCH

If you want to become a professional church grumbler, not just some amateur occasionally throwing rocks at the worship service, minister, or other attributes of the church, there's one key phrase you need to know:

"I'm not being fed."

This simple complaint—the teaching is lacking, the sermons are thin, the worship music is not uplifting enough, or a million other things that people find inadequate—is the official complaint of church grumblers the world over. If we could figure out a way to monetize it, we could permanently end world poverty. Forget cold fusion; if we could generate energy every time someone says this phrase, we'd be able to break our dependence on foreign oil in about four minutes.

It's such a perfect thing to say because it deflects any attention away from me, while at the same time creating false humility and making me seem spiritually mature and advanced. "It's not you, it's me. I just want to learn. I'm admitting that I am incomplete. I'm hungry for deep, real spiritual teaching. I'm humbly confessing that I'm not getting enough out of church. Please help me get the rich faith-building experiences that I so desperately need."

Just be careful who you say this to. Pastors are starting to get wily. When people tell my friend, "I'm not being fed," he replies, "I'm perfectly happy to spoon feed my one-year-old. But if I'm still spoon-feeding him when he's five, we've got a problem. Here's a fork. Feed yourself."

WATCHING R-RATED MOVIES ... BUT ONLY IF THEY'RE VIOLENT

For Christians, it's completely okay to watch R-rated movies, but only if they got that rating because of violence. If they're rated

R because someone is getting their head cut off or there's a battle scene that's so gory, blood splashes on the camera lens, don't worry. God's cool with that. However, if the movie is rated R because of sexuality ... well, I hope you enjoy your fold-out couch bed in hell. It's gonna be a hot one, my friend. A hot one, indeed.

I'm not sure where this rule came from, but it's true. Not only do Christians watch violent R-rated movies, we'll quote them from the pulpit, build sermon series around them—even show clips from them during service. I call it The *Braveheart* Rule, and my theory is that it's because of the Old Testament.

Have you ever read any of the Old Testament? It's hardcore. Samson smashes people in the head with a donkey jawbone. A priest runs a spear through two people having sex. David carries Goliath's head around like a bowling ball. It's violent. I think that Christians read that and assume, "Cool. God's down with some wanton violence. R-rated movies, here we come!"

But if there's any nudity, if a single nipple makes a cameo at any point, forget it. Throw that piece of nonsense in the trash. That is horrible. We'll have to wait until they show the edited version on TBS.

JUDGING FUNDAMENTALISTS FOR BEING JUDGMENTAL

You know what I don't like about fundamentalist Christians? They're so judgmental. I really don't like when people do that. Don't they know we're supposed to be about love and not judgment? Jesus called us to love him with all our heart and all our mind and all our soul. And to love others! Don't they get that? It's about love!

I'm just so sick of their negative attitudes.

They hate dancing too. Did you know that? I'm not making that up or perpetuating a stereotype. They all hate dancing.

They even made a documentary about it one time starring John Lithgow and Hollywood's Kevin Bacon. Gripping stuff really, but I doubt any fundamentalists saw it because they hate popular culture. Ugh, I can barely stand how judgmental they are.

You know they don't drink alcohol, right? Oh no, don't ever offer them a glass of wine or a pint of beer. They'll throw that right back in your face. That's kind of a litmus test I use to determine whether you're a fundamentalist or not. If I suggest we have a glass of red wine and you refuse, then I know. I know exactly what you're all about and I can read the depths of your spiritual walk just by that simple refusal. You're a fundamentalist and you're judgmental.

Sure, I don't know many fundamentalists personally, because I can't stand being around people who are judgmental, but I caught a few seconds of a church service on television once. I think it was a church in Texas. Most fundamentalists either live in Texas or are planning to move to Texas at some point in their lives. But even though I haven't been to a fundamentalist church in, I don't know, ever, you don't need to go to one to know what they're all about. Fire, brimstone, and above all, being judgmental.

Don't you just hate how judgmental fundamentalists are?

I wish they were more open-minded.

BREAKING UP WITH YOUR SMALL GROUP

Many Christians reach a point in their small group relationship where they realize, "This isn't working for me anymore. I need to see other small groups."

It's a tricky situation, fraught with unique challenges. Do you take the passive-aggressive route—just stop showing up? Make excuses until eventually they stop calling? Can you skip group without looking like you're skipping God, because you still love *him*, right? Do you organize a mutiny and try to take other couples with you? "I can't keep studying the book of Job. I'm making a break for it; we're starting a new group and heading to the border of the New Testament. I think we've got room for two other people in our car. Three if someone will sit in the way back, but Hank and Stacy aren't going to be able to make it. Don't look back. Just run. Run!"

Do you work hard to make *them* want to dump *you*? When you host it at your house, do you serve the most disgusting dessert possible, kidney strawberry pie or blackberry beet pudding? Do you start oversharing at group until eventually they ask you to leave out of awkwardness? "I want to talk about some bowel issues I'm having. Anyone else know what I'm talking about? Bowel issues? Here are some detailed observations I had in the bathroom this morning. I took pictures." Do you bring your own poetry and tell people, "God laid this fourteen-page poem about the death of my cat on my heart; I'd really like to read it to you tonight. It's written in Klingon, so it might be a little hard to understand the first time around."

Do you start seeing other groups on the side? And do you keep your broken group going because you like talking about football with one of the guys and your wife likes the recipes one of the girls gives her? You can find substance elsewhere. Just start small grouping all over town until you find one you like, and once you do, you can dump the old one.

If all else fails, I guess you could just be honest. But that's only if you don't know a good recipe for pork pineapple white chocolate chip cookies. People hate those things. Serve a warm plate of those to your small group and it will be over by bite two.

SENDING MORE HATE MAIL
THAN SATANISTS

I'm not going to lie to you. I don't know the exact numbers on this study. There were no Bunsen burners or beakers or statistical flow models plotting percentage of hate mail sent by satanists vs. percentage of hate mail sent by Christians. But I can say without a doubt that when it comes to the hate mail I've had emailed or posted online about things I've written, 100 percent of it has not come from satanists and the majority has come from fellow Christians.

That feels backwards. I don't have any friends who vocally worship satan, to whom I give the middle finger of grammar with a lowercase s, but I assume that there's a lot of hate involved. I have to imagine that when you serve the father of lies there's a lot of lying and criticism and outright nastiness in all forms. Hate for satanists is kind of like Frisbee for Christians. It's just something you do when you sign up. And yet the most frustrated, hope-you-fall-in-a-deep-hole-full-of-cougars-on-crystal-meth hate mail I get is from other Christians.

Which makes no sense. After all, love is right there in our bylaws. We're supposed to love God, love our neighbor, and love ourselves. Pretty simple, but maybe that's too hard to try all at once.

What if this year we set our sights on something reasonable, like, "Let's send less hate mail than devil worshippers"? I admit, that might not be the kind of goal you can slap on the bottom of a Thomas Kinkade poster and sell at craft fairs, but at least it's attainable. I hope.

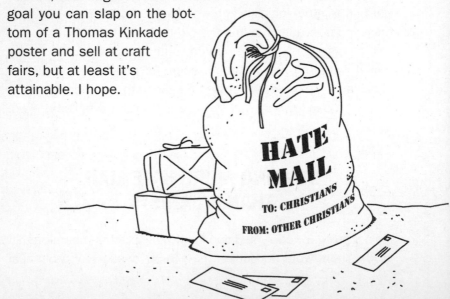

BOYCOTTING YOU UNLESS YOU MAKE
BUTTERY-SOFT T-SHIRTS

Dang you, American Apparel! Ten years ago we would have boycotted you back to the Stone Age. Ask Kmart. We would have risen up against your suggestive advertising and probably had a good old-fashioned product bonfire. There would have been billboards and picketing and yelling, but when it comes to you, we can't muster up a boycott. Your shirts are just so soft and comfortable!

And it's not like you're shy about what you do. We know about how you've used *Penthouse* magazine covers as décor in your stores. We know that when you realized your anti-sweatshop messaging wasn't increasing revenue, you made a deliberate decision to sell using sex. In *Fast Company* magazine your CEO, Dov Charney, was honest enough to say, "That's the problem with the anti-sweatshop movement. You're not going to get customers walking into stores by asking for mercy and gratitude. If you want to sell something, ethical or otherwise,... appeal to people's self-interest."

We tried to dismiss that last part; you can define "self-interest" a lot of different ways, but then the author of that article confirmed our fears:

"Sure, he [the CEO of American Apparel] hoped quality or social consciousness or a distaste for logos would each attract some consumers. But he also hoped that selling a sexed-up version of youth culture to young people would attract others, and hopefully in greater numbers."*

Dang you, American Apparel! I was ready for the boycott, I was, but then the last six T-shirts I got from Christian ministries were printed on American Apparel merchandise, and each one was more comfortable than the last.

Can you at least let us pretend that, when we place an order via cafePress or another printing press, the owner calls you and

---

*Rob Walker, "American Apparel's New Image," *Fast Company* 126 (June 2008).

lets you know that we're reaching out to you in love and that our purchase is actually kind of a witnessing tactic? Will you give us that?

If not, please know that when I put on an American Apparel T-shirt I don't think about the financial support I'm giving a sex-based marketing machine. I think to myself, "I am being *in* this T-shirt, but not *of* this T-shirt." And dang, it is buttery soft!

FEELING SAD FOR CHURCHES THAT AREN'T MEGA

Christians sometimes like to feel small, quiet waves of pity for any church that doesn't have skyrocketing attendance numbers.

That's why every time my wife and I drive by the small Baptist church near my neighborhood on Sunday mornings on the way to the megachurch we attend, I think: Shouldn't the camera crew or the guy who runs the laser show be at church by now? The parking lot is empty at 8:00. Granted it only holds about forty cars, but shouldn't the host team be there already to get the traffic cones set up? Who is going to turn on all the flat screen televisions or get the crane they use for simulcasting the service to other campuses in the right position? Then I remember, that's right, they don't have a crane or other campuses.

And then I feel sad for them.

If God were really happy with what they were doing, wouldn't they have a building as big as the one I go to church in? Wouldn't they have 15,000 on an average Sunday? Wouldn't they have a staff of 400 instead of 4? Wouldn't God bless that church and make it mega if he were pleased with what they were doing?

He would, and that's pretty much what the Bible teaches. In Luke 15:10 it says, "I tell you, there is rejoicing in the presence of the angels of God over one sinner who repents." I know what you're thinking, "Oh, one person is mega to God." But maybe that "one person" is God math, just like some people will argue that six days of creation could equal the human equivalent of 6,000 days. Maybe we're supposed to interpret "one person" as "one greater metro area."

It can all be very confusing. And I'd love to get some wise counsel on it from my small neighborhood church, but I don't even think they have a New Testament specialist on staff. I'm actually pretty convinced that the pastor is also the guy who mows the lawn. Which is so small you couldn't even hold a night out at the movies event on it. How sad.

HATING ON MEGACHURCHES

I attend a megachurch, which means that occasionally, Christians who like to discount the validity of a large church will debate with me why megachurches suck. People don't ever come out and say, "Megachurches suck," but sometimes I wish they did, because it would be a much shorter monologue than this:

> Here's the thing. If a caravan of school buses came to our church one Sunday, thousands of visitors just showed up out of the blue, I'd turn them away. Right then and there, I'd say, "No thanks, we don't want to be a megachurch. Go on, get out of here." I'd probably have to turn on the hose

to chase off the stubborn ones, but the last thing I want to do is attend a megachurch.

I am pretty sure God is not happy with those churches. The music is too loud and the service feels like a concert. Without any hymns I'm not really even sure that counts as a time of worship. You can't form real relationships with people when you're surrounded on a Sunday morning by four thousand other members.

And they use lasers. God hates lasers. And in the great commission, in Matthew 28:19 where it says, "Therefore go and make disciples of all nations," Jesus didn't mean "all" as in everyone. He meant all as in "all the people that can fit in an appropriately sized building." What's an appropriately sized building? The one my church is currently in, and don't go getting any ideas about attending. I've got a hose and I'm not afraid to use it.

OCCASIONALLY SWEARING

Christians occasionally swear. They don't do it a lot. I'm not talking about thirty-second tirades laced with profanity. I just mean that every few days they'll say a swear in the middle of a conversation. Why do we do it? I think we want you to know that we know those words exist. We want you to be aware that we are aware they are out there and we know what they mean. Plus, everyone knows that swears are nineteen times more powerful coming out of the mouth of a Christian. That's a scientific fact right there. If you're a nonbeliever and swear a ton, it's just not that big of a deal. If you're a Christian though and you swear, birds fall out of the sky. Trees shake to their roots. Magma gets fourteen degrees cooler under the crust of the earth. Wielding that kind of power is too tempting to ignore.

SAYING SOMEONE IS GOING TO HAVE A BIGGER HOUSE IN HEAVEN THAN YOU

Every Christian has a slightly different idea of what heaven is going to be like. But the one thing that is consistent is that chances are, someone you know who is super holy is probably going to have a nicer house than you. You're good, but you probably know people whom God is going to take extra special care of when it's all over.

That's why I hope I get to visit my neighbor, Lynn, in heaven. She's definitely going to be in a gated community. I'm sure the gate will be unlocked, because it's heaven and no one is breaking in, but she'll probably still have to buzz me in or maybe trumpet me in. I assume there's a lot of trumpets and harps in heaven.

Don't get me wrong, I'll have a nice place in heaven too, but I've never roofed someone's house after a storm. I've never let my mother-in-law move in with us and nursed her through an illness for a year. I've never babysat my granddaughter two days a week for two years just because that was the right thing to do.

If things continue the way they are, I'll probably have a loft. It will be small, but it will have a nice view, of Lynn's house mostly, because it's going to be so huge it will be hard to be anywhere in heaven and not see it. I'm just saying, she's going to get hooked up.

BEING SLIGHTLY LESS NICE THAN MORMONS

Have you ever met a Mormon who was a jerk? I haven't. Every Mormon I've ever met has been nice, friendly, and well dressed. But I know they have them. Surely someone in Utah is a jerk. But for my money, Mormons are slightly nicer than Christians.

And here's why: Sometimes when jerks become Christians, it's like a bully learning karate. Instead of having Christ transform our hearts and attitudes, we now have a new method with which to beat you up. Our formerly judgmental personality is now backed up by a newfound spirituality. What was once just "forcing everyone to agree with my opinion" is now "forcing everyone to agree with my opinion in the name of God."

HAVING A SPIRITUAL EXCUSE NOT TO HAVE A SPIRITUAL DISCIPLINE

Saying "I don't feel led" is the greatest way to get out of a Christian chore, like having a daily quiet time. Which, by the way, shouldn't feel like a chore. It should feel like an uncontainable desire to spend time with the Lord. You should jump out of bed each morning and throw open your Bible with the gusto of a hungry man at a buffet. Or that's how you think everyone else feels about doing quiet time, except you. They're all excited about it, but not you—you're some sort of grumpy sinner-heathen-pagan.

So to assuage that guilt of not having a consistent quiet time, you'll say, "I don't want to just go through the motions with my quiet time. I want it to be heartfelt, not just something on my to-do list."

That's a great excuse for a number of reasons. First of all, it makes you sound holy. "Wow, this guy is so passionate about spending time with God that he's not going to just phone in his quiet time. He's going to wait until he's truly motivated."

Second, it's one of those lies that if you say it often enough, you eventually start to believe it yourself: "That's right. I *do* love spending time with God, and the best way to show that is by not spending time with him until my heart is right. I want to be on fire for God and not fake it. Until I'm sincere, I'll respect him enough to avoid him."

THINKING YOU'RE SUPPOSED TO GO INTO FULL-TIME MINISTRY

As a Christian, you're obligated to think about going into full-time ministry at least once every three years.

The first time this thought hits you is on your second church retreat. Some people assume that it's during your first retreat, but they're wrong. Especially if the retreat is to a camp where other churches all meet. During that retreat, if you're a boy, your primary thought is, "Will I be able to be that guy in my youth group who makes out with girls from other youth groups?" At least that was my thought. And if you're a girl, you're thinking, "I wish the pastor's son wasn't such a jerk." Or at least the girls in my youth group were thinking that. Mostly because I was.

But on your second retreat you'll get a little nudge, a spiritual bump, and it's going to be pretty tempting to interpret that as the call to ministry. That's probably not what you've received though; you've just received the call to thinking about the call to ministry. And we all get that. So you fight it through high school, tell all your friends you'd never be a pastor, avoid living in Africa as a missionary, and eventually make it to your mid-twenties.

And here it comes again. You start to think about how awesome it would be to go into full-time ministry. Reading the Bible all day and worshipping God at work. You'd never feel frustrated or bored because you'd constantly be doing exactly what you were handcrafted by God on high to do. Then you meet a minister your age. And he's all stressed out and having a difficult time making room for God in his life and you think, "What? You're a professional Christian. You're not supposed to struggle with the things I struggle with." But he does, so you stop thinking about going into the ministry full time.

The urge quiets for a few years and then you get some jerk for a boss. And you think, "I wish God was my boss. That would be awesome. He wouldn't care about my sales sheet. He would care about my soul sheet." Then you feel a little embarrassed because that was such a low-quality joke. And you get a little grumpy. You tell your friends, "I think God is calling me into full-time ministry. This job can't be what my life is all about. There has to be more to life than this. I need to be serving God with my talents full time."

Which is a good thing to say except one of your friends is going to be that guy who says, "We're all in full-time ministry. We should all be serving God full time. Regardless of where you are, you should be worshipping God and reaching people." He's right, but that's still no fun to hear, especially if he loves his job. It's horrible when people who love their job tell you how much you should love yours, and then they bring God into the conversation as further proof of how you're blowing it.

That doesn't make you want to go into full-time ministry. You can't even get your ministry popping at the job you already have. If you can't witness to the people you work with right now, how are you supposed to go into full-time ministry? So the urge fades away again.

But then you hear a really convincing minister or read a book with the word "dream" in the title and you think, maybe, just maybe. And then ...

TRYING NOT TO COMPLAIN AROUND MISSIONARIES

There are two things you need to know about missionaries:
1.   You should always support them.
2.   You should never complain around them.

The first one is pretty obvious; they need our money and our prayers to go serve wherever it is God has called them. The second one is a little more subtle but equally true.

Because even if your missionary friend is quiet and never judgmental, I have to suspect that when you say, "My hot water heater broke and I had to take a cold shower this morning," he's secretly thinking, "Water? I remember water. It's that wet stuff that comes out of pipes sometimes, right? I saw a picture of it in *the* book we have in the desert schoolhouse I teach in, and it reminded me that I had not yet taken a shower this month. But perhaps I will walk into the city next week and see if one of our host families will empty a plastic bottle of gray-colored water on my head. That would be nice, I think. What was that you were saying about your hot water heater? You had to call a plumber after you looked up his number on the internet while eating a sandwich in your house that didn't have snakes regularly coming in through the holes in the wall? No please, go on, I am riveted by this tale of survival and hardship you are spinning, much like the black widow spiders I routinely sweep off my dirt floor or 'bed' if you will. Please do go on."

UGH, MY VENTI, TRIPLE-SHOT, HALF SPLENDA, HALF VANILLA SYRUP, NON-FAT LATTE HAS A PINCH OF CINNAMON IN IT. I WANTED A *SMIDGE*, NOT A *PINCH!*

DEVELOPING SUBTLE SIGNALS TO LET PEOPLE KNOW YOU'RE A CHRISTIAN

I once worked with a guy named Matt who had a really long goatee and a shaved head. For some reason I assumed that meant he hated Jesus. Maybe if his goatee had been a few inches shorter I would have assumed he was indifferent to Jesus, but given the three or four inches of goatee, I was pretty convinced he was violently opposed to Christianity.

One day though, I felt like God was prompting me to talk with him about my faith. In situations like that I usually try to prayer-whisper back to God, "What? Oh come on. I'm at work. I know you're all-knowing and all that, but can you not see the length of his facial hair from up there? He doesn't want to hear about you." But he kept pressing, so I eventually asked Matt what books he had been reading lately. He rattled off a few and then returned the question to me.

In a split second I googled my head for a Christian book title that didn't sound too holy. I instantly landed on Donald Miller's *Blue Like Jazz*. The title is perfect. It sounds like a book about jazz or poetry or perhaps jazz poetry. And I assumed that someone with a goatee that long might like both of those things. So I replied, "I really like the book *Blue Like Jazz*."

He turned in his seat and smiled, "I love that book. My wife is a Christian author and we both really enjoy Donald Miller's writing style." Over the next few months we became friends and shared our faith with each other openly.

What did I *think* would happen? That perhaps upon hearing the word *Christian* Matt would think of every bad image of Christianity he had, the screaming protests, the musicals, the faith-based hand soaps, and throw them right on me?

When my cousin Martha moved to Brooklyn she deliberately wore her Young Life T-shirt on the subway in the hopes that another Christian would recognize the ministry and strike up a conversation with her. It was kind of her way of drawing half the

Jesus fish symbol in the sand the way that persecuted Christians would back in the ancient times to find another believer without getting in trouble.

My hope is that this book will become some sort of weird witnessing tool because it's pretty subtle. Not sure about a friend's view of Christianity? Show him this book. If he says, "Ugh, I hate Christians. They're so judgmental," then flip to the essay titled, "Being Slightly Less Nice Than Mormons" and tell him, "This author thinks that too. You'll love this book." If he replies, "I'm a Christian too," keep this page open and show him these exact words and then write me an email that says, "You just blew my mind, Jonathan Acuff," because I did.

BEING SLIGHTLY OFFENDED THAT THE PASTOR HAS A NICER CAR THAN YOU DO

Christians like their pastors humble, and by humble I mean driving a domestically made mid-sized sedan with high mileage.

I'm not saying I want my pastor to be poor, just that my assumption is that to be a man of the cloth means the seats in your car shouldn't be made of leather. I'm fine if you have a luxury car, if it was a gift from a church member who happens to own a car dealership. Otherwise, I want to be honest, if I see you driving around in a tricked-out Mercedes-Benz, my first two thoughts are going to be:

1. I guess that pastor hates starving children in Africa.
2. I had no idea my tithe was going directly to the procurement of rims.

I want you in a hooptie, not a whip. I want you on a donkey, not a Denali. I want you to know the moral fortitude that comes with having to push a car off the side of the road at least twice a year when it breaks down.

Me? What am I driving? Whoa, let's get back on topic; you're the Varsity Christian, not me. If God chooses to bless me with a Rolls Royce, should I refuse that? Would Abraham or Solomon have scoffed at God's gifts? Think of the great witnessing I can do simply by driving down the highway with spinning rims. Think of the lives that will be touched and transformed when I pull up to a red light and make an automotive declaration, a vehicular proclamation if you will, to the goodness and graciousness of God.

But pastors? You better keep it low key.

#28

Rob Bell

GIVING OURSELVES LIBERAL DEFINITIONS
OF THE PHRASE "QUIET TIME"

Christians try. We try so hard to get this one right, but it just keeps slipping through our fingers. We want to have a steady, regular, consistent, God-is-happy-with-us quiet time, but it's such an on-again, off-again rollercoaster. This is it though. We're getting serious this time. That sermon we heard on Sunday drove home the point that we need a daily quiet time.

The pastor didn't actually say that phrase. He said "personal worship," or maybe "private discipline." He said one of those phrases because "quiet time" sounds kind of churchy and old-fashioned. Regardless, we need one. Some time to be still with God and read our Bible and pray. So we committed. For the next thirty days, it is so *on*. I can't wait. This time's going to be different!

Day one. Monday is theoretically a good day to start my new thirty-day quiet time commitment, but this Monday happens to fall in the middle of the month. Who starts things on the sixteenth of the month? New things should be started at the beginning of the month, or if you really want to ensure success, the beginning of the year. That's the money date right there, January 1. I wish it wasn't October 16th. Nothing good has ever been started on October 16th. Should I wait ten weeks to start my quiet time in the New Year? Probably not. Okay Monday, let's do this.

Day two. Day one was easy. I just started in Genesis and read a little and prayed before work. It's got to be during the morning. There's something doubly Christian about mornings, and if I miss that time, my whole day is shot. God is not cool with me doing my quiet time during lunch or in the early afternoon, and certainly not at night. God is an early bird; satan is a night owl. Everyone knows that.

Day three. Ugh, day three was harder. I just couldn't get up today and slept through my quiet-time hour. I managed to read a Bible verse online when I got to work though. And I said a little prayer to God in the elevator when I came into the building. That's still a pretty good quiet time. Streak unbeaten. Three days down, twenty-seven to go.

Day four. I don't know if you can technically be quiet and listening to a sermon at the same time, but that's what I did for my quiet time today. There was just so much going on at work that I had to come in early. So instead of praying or being still or anything like that, I just listened to a podcast of a sermon while I filed some reports. It was hard to concentrate, but occasionally I would hear the minister say words like "God" and "Jesus," and I would perk up and put the filing down at work for a minute. Take that, day four.

Day five. God loves music. I'm pretty sure David used to sing in the book of Psalms. And they were always lifting their voices to him in the temple. I don't know if Jesus and the disciples ever jammed around the campfire at night though. Maybe they had a harp or something. Did the disciples play harps, or is that only angels? A harp is a really hard instrument to transport unless it's a mini angel harp. I should look that up, but I haven't been able to get very far in Matthew yet. I wanted to today, but traffic was worse than I expected. So I prayed in the car and listened to some of my favorite worship music. God is a fan of Steve Fee and Chris Tomlin, so I'm marking that down as quiet time. Five days!

Day six. Do the weekends count? Do I really need to sit still and listen and pray and read my Bible for it to be considered an official quiet time? I played with my kids a lot this weekend, and God gave them to me and wants me to be a good father, so I'm counting our game of wiffle ball as quiet time. Hooray for six days!

Day seven. God made me unique. He handcrafted me to respond to this world in special, beautiful ways. And one of the things he gifted me with is an appreciation for college basketball. What joy that brings to my heart. How I cry out to the heavens, "Go, Tar Heels!" They played last night and it was a

special time for God and me to share, as we both watched ath-
letes he has gifted with tremendous dunking ability soar about
the floor with grace and beauty. Plus, during a timeout, I looked
out the window and saw a bush, which reminded me of God's
glory and nature and all that. So that makes seven days in a
row doing a quiet time.

This is going to be a lot easier than I thought.

Day 23.

SUBTLY FINDING OUT IF YOU DRINK BEER TOO

If you're a Christian who drinks a beer after mowing the lawn or has a glass of red wine with dinner, there's a sneaky little game you play when you meet new Christians. It's called, "Do These Christians Drink Too?"

The reason you play this game is not that you're afraid of looking bad in front of people who don't drink. I have friends who choose not to drink, and they never get on me about having a beer. They never try to choke-hold me for drinking wine. Not at all. But there are people who will leg drop you if they find out you drink. They'll say things like, "I really think all the bad things that happen to you are because God is punishing you for starting to have mixed drinks." That's a real quote. From a friend.

There's never been a good way to smoke these people out, a guide, as it were, to find out who's going to punch you in the face with judgment and who's going to love you, regardless of what you're drinking . . . until now.

This is the Official *Stuff Christians Like* Subtle Guide to Finding Out If Another Christian Drinks Too. (The OSCLSGTFOIACDT, if you will):

The Anything

When you're going to visit someone's house, call a few days beforehand and offer to "bring anything you need, like drinks." Make sure you stress the word *anything* over and over again. What's so great about this technique is that it puts the pressure back on them. Now they're faced with the decision to ask you to bring wine or Sprite.

The Garage Poke

Studies show that 78 percent of all Christians hide their beer in the garage when people they don't know will come over. Okay, I conducted the study myself, but trust me, it's true. Make up an excuse to go to the garage and then poke around. Don't snoop. Snooping is what the lady on *Murder, She Wrote* did. Just poke. There's a huge difference.

The Keychain

This one is easy to execute. Just look at their keychain. If they have a bottle opener on it, you're all set. No one ever drinks enough old-timey soda to need a bottle opener around all the time. Speaking of soda, bring over a six pack of old-school soda as a housewarming gift. Make sure you bring bottles with tops that won't unscrew. Then watch carefully to see what they do next. Do they instantly go to the drawer where the bottle opener is? Do they seem familiar with this task? Does it fit the contour of their hand easily from years of usage? Is there a picture of Bud Light's dog, Spuds Mackenzie, on the opener, indicating that it is a trusted friend dating back to the mid-eighties?

The Traveler

One of my favorite places on the planet is the Garage Cafe & Bar in Birmingham, Alabama. It's an antique store built out of old horse stalls, with a huge open courtyard that spills a sea of statues and period furniture under a blanket of white Christmas lights and dark sky. At night, it's a beautiful place to have a beer and feel poetic. If I tell you that story and the only words you hear are "bar" and "beer," then chances are we feel different about drinking. Tell a story about a place you've visited and see if the first reaction is, "A bar? You went to a bar? Do you think you'll be in the hot part of hell or the wicked-hot part?"

I guess at the end of the day you could just quit playing games with their heart and ask them directly: "Did you know Sam Adams Summer Ale has grains of paradise in it? It's a spice that someone felt deserved the name 'grains of paradise.' That's like building a car and naming it 'super duper awesome bestest car in the world.' Do you enjoy premium beer like I do?"

SECRET CHRISTIAN BANDS

It must not be easy to be a Christian band these days. When you say, "We're a Christian band," people probably ask you things like, "Really? Which one of you is in charge of releasing the doves during your performance?" Or, "Do you take a love offering before you rock or after you rock?" Or, "How many of your songs discuss punching the devil directly in the face? Half ... or all?"

There's gotta be *some* downside to being labeled a Christian band because an entire underground of secret Christian bands has developed over the last fifteen years. I don't know where they came from, but occasionally while you're listening to the radio or watching the television show *So You Think You Can Dance*, your friend will lean over and whisper quietly, "Those guys are Christian." Or *Rolling Stone* will "out them" in a review of their record and ask nine God-flavored questions and one album question in an interview.

We all know they're out there, but what does it take to become one? What if you're a budding musician with deep faith who wants to quietly join the underground Christian band movement? Here's how you can secretly apply for membership:

Name yourself something that sounds "longing" but not "Lordly."

I love the band name "Demon Hunter," but there's no pretending they're not a Christian band. It's like naming your band, "satan Groin Kickers." Way, way too obvious. Try to shoot for something middle of the road. "Staind" would be a great name if it weren't already taken. Do they mean they're "staind" as in damaged beyond repair? Or do they mean they're "staind" as in covered by the blood of Jesus? Aim for something like that. It should be melancholy but also possibly uplifting if viewed through the filter of grace. And on a side note, I'm pretty sure bands like "Staind" are the reason extra "e's" started showing up in all our church names, like Crosspointe, Lifepointe, Truth-pointe, etc. Maybe we traded them some amps for their e's.

Learn how to answer the question, "Are you a Christian band?"

At some point, this is going to come up, and you have to be ready. When anyone asks, answer, "No, we're not a Christian band. We're a band of Christians." I love this one because it works on so many levels outside of music. "Are you a Christian ultimate Frisbee team? No, we're an ultimate Frisbee team of Christians." See? Isn't that nice? The circular logic of this will usually baffle people enough that you can quietly slip out of the room. If it doesn't, just tell them you're a guild, not a band. They'll assume you're quoting *Lord of the Rings*, and then you can talk about New Zealand for the rest of the night. Which I hear is a lovely place.

Write songs about your girlfriend *and* God.

All your lyrics should be interchangeable so that if people in the audience want to pretend you're singing about God, they can. If they want to pretend you're singing about your girlfriend, they can. For example: "Your love has opened up a part of me I didn't know I had / Without you in my life, my days would be so sad." That's magical, right? Maybe a girlfriend changed that singer's life . . . or maybe God did. Hard to tell, especially since you strip all the pronouns out. Tricky. (By the way, if you want to use that lyric, you can. That's yours for free. Keep that one somewhere safe.) Before you know it, your fans will be saying to each other, "I love this song because it reminds me of this girl I dated in high school *and* also my life-redeeming relationship with the Lord."

THROWING OUT VERBAL CANARIES

Lean in close and I'll tell you a little secret. Sometimes, Christians throw out ideas when we're with other Christians to see if they will judge us for something we secretly like. We'll say, "Yeah, this guy I know went to that new nightclub and said it was crazy." Then, we'll pause and observe their reaction. If they say, "Dancing is evil. I hate nightclubs and so does God," we immediately agree with them, "Amen. God wants to smite them. Probably use sulfur, if I had to guess." But if they say something like, "Let's go check it out," we'll respond, "I've heard that place is good too. We should go sometime."

It's kind of like how coal miners used to have a canary down in the shaft with them. If the bird died, something was wrong with the air quality. Well, what we do is introduce a verbal canary. Then, if someone kills it, we can still look holy and say something like, "Yeah, that bird sucked anyway."

TREATING THE STREET CORNER PREACHER LIKE A PIÑATA

We have a love/hate relationship with that street corner preacher who yells about repentance on the sidewalks of cities around the world. We love to use him as a sermon illustration of how *not* to do God and church and the gospel. And we hate that we get lumped in with him when someone says, "I don't like Christianity. It's so judgmental and screamy." It's true, you're not an official street corner preacher unless you're sweaty and have a sign with all caps and an abundance of exclamation points and at least one mention of satan or hell.

The challenge, though, is that the repent message—the "get your stuff together; it's about to get real" message that street corner preachers proclaim—is actually the first sermon Jesus gave. Matthew 4:17 says, "From that time on Jesus began to preach, 'Repent, for the kingdom of heaven is near.' " That verse doesn't elaborate or tell us the rest of his message. There's the sense that this was his entire sermon, like it was written on a sign: *REPENT!!!!! FOR THE KINGDOM OF HEAVEN IS NEAR!!!!!*

USING WATERFALLS AND BUTTERFLIES AS AN OPPORTUNITY TO GIVE EVOLUTIONISTS THE MIDDLE FINGER

Regardless of the specifics you believe about the creation of the earth—God did it in six literal days; "days" meaning something different in his economy; he set things in motion that have grown and changed over time according to his plan, etc.—you're required by Christian law to sarcastically proclaim, "And it was all an accident!" when you encounter something amazing in nature.

Whether it's a beautiful mountain range, an ocean ecosystem functioning perfectly in a tidal pool, or the birth of a child, you have to let everyone you're with know that God created it. And the smarmier you can be about it the better. Sure, you could always just say, "I personally believe God created this," but where's the fun in exclaiming that?

It's much better to say, "And it was all an accident." Not only do you give God a quiet little shout-out, you also get to say, "How dumb are people who believe in evolution and the big bang and a million other ideas?" Which is completely in line with Jesus' whole "love your neighbors through sarcasm" thing. I think that's in the book of Mark. I'd look it up, but the sun is rising right now in my office, and tender beams of light are tickling trees thick with leaves that seem to stand sentinel to the approaching morning; it is gorgeous, and it was all an accident.

FEELING SLIGHTLY DISAPPOINTED WHEN SOMEONE ACCEPTS OUR FAKE OFFER OF GENEROSITY

Christians find it nice to tell someone, "Please let me know if there's anything I can do for you. Anything at all." Especially if that person recently experienced a tragedy or is about to set out on some big adventure that will clearly require the help of others. It feels good to write that blank check of support. Plus, as a Christian, we're probably supposed to say that. I don't know if that exact phrase is in the Bible, but I'm sure there's something close to that in the New Testament. But what if someone calls your bluff? What if in the midst of enjoying that really warm feeling of fictional support, someone tries to take you up on the offer? That's bogus, right?

For bad people, that is. Not you and me of course, but for people who say, "Please let me know if there's anything I can do for you" and don't really mean it. That happens you know. I know you and I always say it without conditions, but some people throw out fake offers of generosity.

It happened to a friend of mine who was going on a mission trip. She spoke at church about the trip and afterward a man approached her to offer his unconditional support. When he asked if there was anything he could do to help her, she said, "I could really use some financial support." He looked her dead in the eye and said, "I'll pray for you."

Good grief. Didn't she know the protocol of the fake support offer? I say, "Please let me know if there's anything I can do for you," and then you say, "I'll let you know; thank you so much for your generosity." Then we go our separate ways and I get to enjoy about 67 percent of what it would feel like if I actually helped you. You're not supposed to take me up on the offer. That's just rude.

But what if you run into someone who doesn't know you're only pretending when you offer support? There's got to be a better approach than just saying, "I'll pray for you." Here are two ideas:

Say, "God gifted me with the spiritual gift of thought, not action." Tell them you'll be thinking about them next Saturday when they struggle to move everything they own across town. No one likes to help people move, but you can't just say, "I hate moving, no thanks," when they ask you to bring your pickup truck over and help out. So instead, try to tell them that your particular spiritual gift involves thinking about solutions to challenges, not actually participating in the solution.

Or, just throw your car keys. It's better to walk home than it is to have someone actually cash your blank check of help. But it doesn't really have to be your car keys, anything shiny will do. That's why I always keep a handful of silver glitter in my pockets. If I get pushed into a conversational corner I throw the glitter into the air, and while the person I'm talking to is distracted, I run away. An additional benefit is that I look like a cool magician, so I've got that going for me.

PRAYER

Fine, I'll say it. I know it's not technically a competition, but if someone says "Yes Jesus" while I am praying instead of just "Yes," I feel a lot better about the quality of my prayer. I know some folks feel that a "grunt of affirmation," a la Master P's hit song "Make 'em say Uhh," is a stronger confirmation of the awesomeness of a prayer, but call me old school; I still think a "Yes Jesus!" that floats up from the backup pray-ers while you do your solo is the best way to earn some major prayer points. Are we still frowning on that kind of thing, or is it acceptable to score prayer now?

SAYING "I'LL PRAY FOR YOU" ...
AND THEN NOT

Sometimes saying "I'll pray for you" is just the Christian equiva-lent of ending a date by saying, "I'll give you a call." It shouldn't be, but it is, and right now I have about a 17 percent success rate when it comes to actually following through on my "I'll pray for you" promises. I know that's horrible, but that reflects a ten-year average that includes 2000 – 2005, when I was batting about .000. I've done better these last five years to pull up my average, but you know what they say about prayer statistics: "It's a marathon, not a sprint." (I think there was an analogy traffic jam in that last paragraph.)

But what if there was a better way? What if instead of say-ing, "I'll pray for you," and then not, we could all do something else? What if we could learn some other ways to end a Christian conversation?

"Here, have some pocket candy."

Conversations, much like Saturday Night Live skits, are often difficult to end. What started out funny and enjoyable just kind of slowly deteriorates until you're both standing there saying, "So ... yeah ... that's what's going on." I think it might be nice, when you sense that a conversation has lost its momentum and it's time to move on, if you offered the person you're talking with some pocket candy. Instead of saying, "I'll pray for you," you could say, "I need to go now, but I'd like to leave you with something. Here, have some pocket candy." Everyone loves candy. And even if they don't, they'll be too stunned to really say anything as you fill their hands with delicious treats, rather than an empty promise to pray for them.

"Razzle dazzle."

This one makes no sense and that's kind of the point. It's just really fun to say, and at the bare minimum, it will be awkwardly funny. Just imagine if your friend says, "So anyway, that's what's going on. Not much else ... whatever," and you reply, "Razzle Dazzle man, Razzle Dazzle." (Bonus points if you can combine this one with pocket candy and actually give your friend a handful of Razzles, the candy that turns into a gum. Remember that stuff? It somehow managed to suck as both a gum and as a candy. Phenomenal.)

"That's interesting."

If you've ever worked in a corporation, you've heard this phrase. This term is so large and undefined that when someone shows you an idea at work, you can say, "That's interesting," and it can mean everything from, "I like that plan! I think we should turn it into a project," to, "That is the worst idea I have ever heard in my life and will probably bankrupt the company if we so much as make eye contact with it." Try it today. You can use it in almost any situation. Someone spills coffee on your computer keyboard: "That's interesting. The vowels don't work anymore." Someone offers you a raise and an office with a door: "That's interesting. I think I would like a promotion." It's great for work, and it's a pretty handy "I'll pray for you" replacement. Not because it's a dishonest phrase, but because it buys you time to gather your thoughts and reflect on the conversation instead of just throwing up an automatic "I'll pray for you."

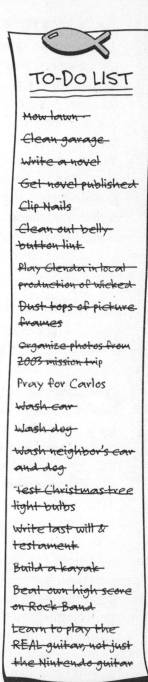

TO-DO LIST

~~Mow lawn~~
~~Clean garage~~
~~Write a novel~~
~~Get novel published~~
~~Clip Nails~~
~~Clean out belly button lint~~
~~Play Glenda in local production of Wicked~~
~~Dust tops of picture frames~~
~~Organize photos from 2003 mission trip~~
Pray for Carlos
~~Wash car~~
~~Wash dog~~
~~Wash neighbor's car and dog~~
~~Test Christmas-tree light bulbs~~
~~Write last will & testament~~
~~Build a kayak~~
~~Beat own high score on Rock Band~~
~~Learn to play the REAL guitar, not just the Nintendo guitar~~

"Let's pray right now."

Rock the PRT (Prayer Right There) if you really want to pray for someone. Don't let the push and pace of life swallow the request. Even if you write down a prayer request, you're going to lose that piece of paper or your wife will throw it away because she thought it was trash even though it also had a great book idea on it. Hypothetically speaking, of course. So just pray. Or if that feels weird, pray while you walk away or drive away or Ruckus away, if you are so lucky to own a Honda Ruckus scooter. (I love that word *ruckus*. That's what I want to do with God—create a ruckus. And the idea of creating a ruckus while at the same time riding a scooter named Ruckus makes my head spin.)

NOT KNOWING IF WE'RE SUPPOSED TO PRAY FOR FRIENDS HAVING PLASTIC SURGERY

I had cosmetic surgery once. I know what you're thinking: pec implants. You've probably seen that beach photo of me that's going around the internet. I didn't want to do it, but when *Guideposts* magazine asks you to be part of their "Hottest Christian Bloggers" calendar, what can you do?

I didn't have pec implants. I got a nose job—or rhinoplasty, if you prefer—when I was eighteen. My dad is a pastor and was a pioneer of "doing things with excellence" for the church. So when my face took a bad turn during high school, he nipped that right in the bud (or septum, as it were) and made sure I was hott with two t's. I completely understand his logic. You think some first-time visitor's going to stick around and give their life to Christ if the pastor's oldest son looks like some kind of gargoyle perched on the front row of the sanctuary?

He'd probably tell you that the surgery was to fix my nose after a horrendous skateboarding accident that left me with a face opposed to breathing, but that's not the point. The point is, are we supposed to pray for someone who is having unnecessary plastic surgery?

Let's pretend you're at small group and your friend says, "I have a prayer request. I'm getting calf implants tomorrow and would really like you guys to lift me up in prayer."

Do you say, "No, I'm not praying for that," right away, or do you dig a little deeper? Maybe you have this conversation:

YOU: Do you *have* to get calf implants? Is this because of some medical condition?

YOUR FRIEND: Yes, it's called "no-tone-leg-itis." I've got a bad case of it. No matter how hard I work out, I just can't get my legs cut up.

YOU: You need a *funny* implant because that joke was horrible. So this is just an aesthetic thing?

YOUR FRIEND: Yes. I want sexy legs. When I walk in the room, I want every eye to be captivated by the beauty of my calves. I'm really nervous about the surgery and going under the knife and all of that.

YOU: I think what you need to be afraid of is those pastel and neon pants that weightlifters wear because their legs are too bulgy for normal pants. They're like MC Hammer pants, just not as classy ... and that's saying something.

YOUR FRIEND: Please just pray that the doctors would have wisdom tomorrow and that everything would go smoothly.

YOU: Oh, no. I can see it now. You're going to be one of those guys who shaves his legs even though he's not an Olympic-level swimmer or cyclist. You're going to shave your arms next. You'll be like this hairless man from the future, with smooth arms, ripped calves, and a fake tan. I don't like where this is going at all.

That's a pretty grim future, my friend. So maybe the answer is yes. Yes, we should pray for our friends who are getting calf implants. Not just for the surgery, but also that they won't turn into a flesh-colored Tron in the weeks that follow their surgery. Focus your prayer there.

JUST USING GOD'S FAVORITE WORD WHEN WE PRAY

For centuries, we Christians have secretly used God's favorite word in all our prayers. To even mention it, I embrace great danger and peril and risk and other words that mean bad things could happen to me. This word, above all others, ensures that God will hear your prayers and answer them quickly and awesomely. To put this powerful word into the hands of non-believers could find me banished to the balcony at church, and everyone knows that the Holy Spirit only touches people on the ground floor during service. But I must share.

I am, of course, speaking of the word *just*. Here's how we use it in prayer:

"Lord, we just pray you will just hear us tonight. We just lift up our hands to you and just pray that you will just send your love down to us in ways we just can't understand. Take us just as we are, Lord. Just, just, just, just."

I added those last four for emphasis, but it's not far from the truth. I'm not sure why we do that, but I should probably apologize. Next time someone prays, you're going to have highly tuned "just radar" and will probably be thinking in your head, "I just hate that book *Stuff Christians Like*."

THE SEVEN PEOPLE YOU MEET IN A PRAYER CIRCLE

Prayer circles can provide some surprisingly tense moments. At church or in a small group, someone will say, "I'll open us in prayer. Lisa, you close us. Everyone else, pray if you feel led."

Suddenly, there's an expectation. In less than a minute, that opening prayer is going to wrap up, and you'll be faced with an incredibly difficult decision: Do I pray? Do I feel led? When do I pray? When is the "Closer" going to speak up and end this thing? How do I not start praying at the same time as someone else?

There are so many questions, each fraught with danger and intrigue. That's why I created this simple list, "The Seven People You Meet in a Prayer Circle." It's like that book, *The Five People You Meet in Heaven*, but slightly more sarcastic and bound not to become a made-for-television movie.

1. The Opener

You might think the Closer is the one with all the power, but don't be misled. The Opener is in control. In addition to often choosing the Closer, they set the tone for the entire prayer circle. If they go long, people after them will go long. If they add cute little jokes to the opening prayer, people after them will be casual too. More than that, they don't have to worry about the Closer or fear someone else cutting them off. They can pray and then relax. Their job is done in a matter of seconds.

2. The Almost-er

This is the person sitting near you who is constantly on the verge of praying. You can hear them doing that little breath thing—that small inhale that occurs a split second before someone speaks. And you can hear it because it's loud in the deafening silence of the prayer circle. Every time you're about to say a prayer, you hear the Almost-er and stop because you don't want to cause a prayer train wreck. And then they don't pray. So you start again, and an inhale from the Almost-er stops you again. It's quite the little dance.

3. The Rambler

Another name for this person is the "Jon Acuff." This is the person who sees the chance to pray in front of people as an open microphone. A chance to not-so-subtly reference everything they've recently learned during their quiet time in one long, rambling prayer that feels like a sermon. And there's no way to stop them, unless you're married to them. If you are, then, like my wife, you can grab the Rambler's hand and give him a squeeze that says, "I love you. You are good at praying, but no one wants to hear about the spiritual mysteries you've uncovered recently in the book of Joel." (It's possible I've Lifetime-channeled my interpretation of that hand squeeze though, and my wife is actually trying to say, "Stop. Please, stop right now. You are killing me with your Bible-flavored rambletastic ridiculousness.")

4. The Cave-In

Deciding not to pray in a prayer circle is like not giving to a love offering. "What? You don't feel led? You're the only person in the room who didn't get led? The Holy Spirit isn't speaking to you right now? Maybe we should pray for you instead of doing this prayer circle." Expect at least one person to be the Cave-In and give in to prayer pressure.

5. The Gunslinger

When there are only two people left who haven't prayed and the Closer is mentally warming up to end the session, you may end up in a prayer showdown. It's just you and one other person who haven't prayed yet. The entire circle senses that the first few prayers were good, but they just need one more tiny prayer to wrap things up before the Closer. But you don't want to pray, and neither does the Gunslinger. So you sit there in silence across from each other, like cowboys in the street, waiting, letting the tension and the awkwardness build, until finally someone draws their gun and blurts out, "Lord, thank you for this day and everything you've blessed us with!"

6. The Shot Blocker

This one is rare. Hearing this in a group prayer is like seeing a unicorn. But it can happen in a prayer circle when everyone in the room knows that someone is praying for something they should *not* be praying for. The entire circle knows that Mark is the wrong guy for Sue and can't resist jumping in after she prays. Here's how it usually goes down:

> SUE: Lord, I just pray that you would continue to strengthen and bless my relationship with Mark.
> SHOT BLOCKER: Lord, please give Sue more patience. Help her to see with clarity. Help her not rush into anything that goes against your plan for her life.

This is the basketball equivalent of someone blocking your shot into another state. Right as the prayer is floating up to heaven, someone swoops in and shot blocks it back down to earth.

7. The Closer

Closing a prayer circle is like being Spider-Man. With great power comes great responsibility. Although you get to determine when it ends, you also have to monitor the amount of quiet time that signifies everyone's had their turn. Because what you don't want to happen—what the Closer fears most—is the "Encore-ist." This is the person who follows the Closer, boldly defying all rules of group prayer. It's an embarrassing situation for a Closer, and for several minutes afterward, it's hard to make eye contact with them.

Those are the seven. I didn't formally include the Encore-ist on the list because even God can't stand that person.

From STUFFCHRISTIANSLIKE.NET

#148 War-Themed Ministries.

FORGETTING TO MENTION SOMEONE'S PRAYER REQUEST WHEN YOU CLOSE A GROUP IN PRAYER

Maybe Christians are inherently forgetful. Sometimes when we share prayer requests, it feels like one of those moments where the waiter at a restaurant really isn't listening to an order. It's always a little uncomfortable when he refuses to write down your meal. Especially if you're dining with someone who regards the menu as a palette of options to *create with* more than a list of meals to *choose from*.

"I'll take the chicken, but cook it as if it's a piece of beef. Instead of a cream sauce, I'll take a red sauce. Instead of rice, I'll have beans. Instead of pine nuts, I'll take walnuts. And instead of capers, could I get a banana split sundae? Could you crumble the croutons to a fine powder over the salad? And please leave every third piece of lettuce on the side of the plate. I'm trying to cut my lettuce intake by at least 33 percent."

When the waiter hears all this and just nods without taking down a single thing on paper, I get nervous. There's no way that dish is coming out the way it was ordered. It's impossible to remember all of that, and my friend might send the meal back—which is awkward for all parties.

As much as I dislike that silly little situation, it's nothing compared to when you're at church or in a small group and one person is assigned to say a massive, include-everyone's-request closing prayer. At this point, they should have a pen and pad out because people are going to fire out prayer requests.

Some will be simple: "I need a new job." Some will be more complicated: "My dad has gout on his big toe, and his brother came into town to help him, and while he was here he stole his baseball card collection, so I need prayer for the toe and the eventual capture of the brother and the safe return of the baseball card collection." If you're not writing them down, the inevitable is going to happen: You'll leave someone out.

"I'm sorry. Your prayer request did not make the cut. Good luck with all that." That's what you essentially say to the one person you forgot to mention. Mary's job request got lifted up. The big toe and the brother and the baseball collection got some love. But you left out one person, and if they're listening, they're probably going to be thinking you just prayer-punked them. So what do you do?

1. You'll put remembering the specifics on God.

Sometimes it's best to just put God in charge of remembering all the details. Pray something like, "God, you've heard everyone's requests tonight. We ask that you remember them and watch over them in your goodness." No one's going to complain that you didn't specifically pray for them, because God's on it.

2. You'll throw out a blanket prayer statement.

I was in a small group once where the guy praying said before he started, "I'm not going to try to remember everyone's prayer request." I liked that. He was realistic and let all of us know up front, "You're not getting any specific shout-outs in this prayer I'm about to give. Deal with it."

If I had to choose, I'd lean toward the last option. At the bare minimum it's honest. But I still think writing them down is the way to go. Sometimes we take prayer requests pretty casually. We treat them like status meetings at work, where people check on how projects are coming along: "The Q1 numbers are up and the vendor has been selected for the accounting issue." But a prayer request is different from a status report. It's you asking someone else to commune with God on your behalf, so it might be one of those rare moments in life where breaking out a pen and a piece of paper is called for.

TRYING TO SAY SOMETHING CHRISTIANY WITHOUT LOOKING LIKE A SNAKE HANDLER

I am slightly terrified that you will think I am a snake-handling Christian. It's not that I'm constantly carrying around squirming burlap bags jam packed with vipers. I don't have any small wounds on my hands and stories that start off like this: "Well, I wasn't prayed up enough and you know what they say about dancing with an eastern diamondback when you're too distracted by the world to focus on the 'bitey' end." I've never even been to a church that considers a rattlesnake a pulpit accessory, but I don't want you to think I'm a weird Christian.

That's why depending on whom I'm talking with, I'll tell the same story using very different words to describe something I feel like God told me.

If I'm with some livin-on-the-edge, completely-sold-out-for-Jesus friends, I'll come right out and say, "God told me _____."

If my friends are a little more conservative, I'll say, "I felt like God said to me _____." Or the "Holy Spirit burdened me with _____." Or "God laid _____ on my heart and impressed on me _____."

If I don't know the people at all and we just met, I might say, "Go Red Sox!"

It's all very confusing, but even sillier than that is when I try to put a spin on the word "sin."

Christians don't like to say the word "sin." We use synonyms because we think that if we say "sin" some folks will label us a traditional old school super Christian Bible belter.

Here are the words we use instead:

junk	struggles
failures	mistakes
baggage	issues
hang-ups	problems
challenges	

I work in the corporate world, where you're supposed to put a spin on bad things. You're supposed to say, "I found an opportunity for improvement," not, "I made a mistake." You should say, "I have identified some growth areas in my performance," not, "I figured out why that project I presented caught on fire in the conference room."

But when Jesus died on the cross he didn't do so because he wanted to "shift my paradigm." He didn't come to help me "realize my full potential" and "unpack my baggage." Or "overcome my hang-ups." Or "recalenderize my Q1."

USING "LET ME PRAY ABOUT IT" AS A EUPHEMISM FOR "NO"

I love when someone asks us to help out at church and instead of saying, "No," we say, "Let me pray about it." Really? I asked you to help me clean up tomorrow night after youth group, and you feel like that's something you need to run past the Savior of the world? He's going to give you the thumbs-up or thumbs-down on whether or not you can help me stack chairs for seven minutes?

CEASING WITHOUT PRAYING

When GE sent me an email to let me know that one of their appliances would be featured on the *Oprah* show, I didn't have a problem unsubscribing from that email list. But it's not so simple if you're a Christian and find yourself on a prayer chain you didn't sign up for.

What's this? The "Nantahala River Prayer Chain?" How did I get on this thing? Do I have a crazy aunt that lives in the Nantahala Gorge area? Or is someone in my small group loosely tied to this ministry and just included all of us on his personal crusade to pray for river people? Is that the politically correct term for "hill people"? Clearly "hillbilly" is no good; I'm going with river people. How many river people are there though, because I'm getting daily reminders to pray for them? Is it one email reminder per river person?

Why is this email chain blowing up all of a sudden? Has there been a new predator introduced into the river? And do we really need to use the bright red Microsoft Outlook "!" of importance with every email? I could understand if you were actually sending this prayer request from an iPhone while in the river, while being bitten by an Alligator Gar, but other than that exact circumstance, it seems a little extreme.

How do I unsubscribe from this prayer chain without making it look like I hate Jesus, prayer, and river people? Should I say that I'm already praying for some river people in my own state? Should I tell them I'm a beach kind of person and feel called to pray strictly for ocean-related people groups? If I donate some money to the cause, can I buy my way off the list? Should I sign up for a new gmail account and tell them my email address changed? I'll still use my current email address for everything but river people–flavored messages. Maybe that's the best plan.

Is there a loving way to unsubscribe from a prayer chain without feeling like you're hitting the "unfaithful" button?

NOT KNOWING WHICH MEALS TO PRAY BEFORE

You don't have to pray before you eat something that has nougat in it. A lot of people don't know this, but if you look deep enough into the Old Testament, you'll find the Hebrew word for nougat: *chonoug.* Most seminaries aren't teaching this information, which is a shame—a dang shame.

These are the kinds of conversations I have with my friends. Especially when it comes to praying before meals. This is such a murky subject that I've created the following guide. Tear it out and keep it in your purse or wallet for the next time you have a question about proper food prayers. ⟶

BEING COMPLETELY TERRIFIED TO PRAY FOR PATIENCE OR HUMILITY

Sometimes, "Have you prayed about that?" is a blanket statement we Christians use when we're a little tired of listening to you talk about a particular problem. It's not that we don't want to hear about it; it's just that you're rambling a little and maybe we've got places to go, so we'll just throw out that question knowing that chances are ... you haven't. And then you can go home and pray, and we can go home and feel like we've shared some godly wisdom.

But there are two things that friends will never encourage each other to pray about. Two topics that are so explosively dangerous that if we ever overhear someone about to pray for them we'll leap through the air, stretching our bodies out horizontally to slap the prayer from their mouth. The dangerous subjects?

Patience and humility.

Even as you read that, you probably chuckled to yourself and thought, "Oh boy, those are two things you don't want God to give you." And you're right. Collectively we've made those the most dangerous things in the world to ask for. I think we're afraid that when we pray for patience and humility, God's going to answer that request with a beard and a barrel.

The beard symbolizes how long you'll have to wait for something you really want. As if the moment you ask God to give you more patience about your job situation, he's going to say, "You got it. Now you can't leave the job you're in for the next thirty-four years. Hope you enjoy that cubicle. Ha, ha. Gotcha, sucker."

Guide to Food Prayers

The Stand Up Rule

If you have to stand up while eating, you don't have to pray. Regardless of what you're eating, standing up makes the food feel very light and insignificant. It's impossible to cut anything while standing, too. You end up just spearing chunks of fruit or meat awkwardly while trying to keep the plate from tipping over onto the carpet, which would further upset the hosts, whose dog you just made urinate on the couch because you got it too excited at the Christmas Eve party and your dad yelled at you. (That just got personal, but trust me, no prayer required here.) Use this easy rhyme to remember: "If you have to stand / God won't demand / a prayer tonight / so take a bite."

Wedding Food

This rule actually works for any big event where one person prays for the whole room. Listen carefully to that person's prayer. If it's good, dig in. If it's a little weak, you'd better double up and pray for yourself, just to be sure. No offense to the other person, but it's better safe than sorry. Plus, it makes you look extra prayerful, which is never a bad thing if you're single and trying to meet a bridesmaid.

Drive In

This actually depends on which fast food restaurant you go to. If you go to Chick-fil-A or In-N-Out you probably don't have to pray because those are Christian restaurants and holiness is pre-applied like barbecue sauce to all the food. You're covered. Taco Bell, Burger King, and other restaurants are questionable. At the bare minimum, turn your back in the car while they use that bean and guacamole gun at Taco Bell and say a prayer. Chances are you'll need it.

Progressive Dinner

A progressive dinner is where you travel with people from house to house, having one course at each. The question is, where and when do you pray? Is it before the first house, or at each house? Good question. I pray at the beginning and then at each house that serves something that might need a little God. When I used to be a bag boy at a grocery store, we called it "spot mopping." You didn't mop the whole floor, just the few areas that required it. Same thing applies here. If one house has a fresh Mandarin spinach salad, hold the prayer. If the next one has some sort of homemade sausage that may or may not be squirrel, you'd better start praying.

Gas Station Snacks

Nougat? No prayer. Beef jerky? Depends. If you do regular jerky, no problem—you don't have to pray. If you do that jerky + cheese marriage thing where there's a tube of orange cheese spooning the jerky, you'd better pray.

Before or after Appetizers

The best way to get a waiter or waitress to come to your table is to start praying. They materialize out of thin air, like some sort of prayer-interrupting phantom. I suggest praying in the parking lot before you even enter the restaurant. That way, you eliminate any possible chance of the staff crashing your prayer party.

The barrel is what you're going to be wearing when God instantly makes you homeless as a way to increase your humility. He's just going to take away everything you have and leave you with only a barrel to wear. And not even a nice one that looks old-fashioned and might have come from a sun-dappled winery in Sonoma, California. I'm talking about a gross old barrel that probably held beets before it held you. Don't expect rope suspenders, either. God's taking those, too. You'll be holding up that barrel with your bare hands.

I'm not sure what our fear of patience and humility really means. Maybe we think God won't notice we need more patience or humility, and he'll forget to slow our lives down or take all our stuff away. We'll be able to skate on through at a normal pace with loads of possessions unless we accidentally summon God with the words "patience" and "humility" like Beetlejuice or the boogeyman.

So if you're feeling like this book isn't funny, either *you* prayed for patience when it came to finding a good book to read, or *I* prayed for humility.

DISGUISING GOSSIP AS PRAYER

We've all either heard somebody do this, or we've done it ourselves: In the middle of a prayer circle, someone will raise their hand with a prayer request and then proceed to gossip about somebody else. Usually it sounds like this:

"I want to lift up my friends Charlie and Sandra. Sandra caught Charlie looking at pornography online, and he yelled at her for running up all their credit cards. And you all probably know their son got kicked out of school for getting drunk and doing the African Anteater Dance from the movie *Can't Buy Me Love* at the homecoming dance. So I really just want to pray for them."

I'm sure that when God hears stuff like that, he wants to throw a lightning bolt down at us. And not just a regular one, but some sort of super lightning bolt coated with tigers and switchblades. But what should you do when someone in your small group disguises gossip as prayer?

I suggest you hit that person with a plank.

I know, that sounds violent. Beating someone with a 2 x 4 chunk of wood about the head, neck, and shoulder regions might seem aggressive at first. But hear me out. I think that when a new small group is forming, they should make a "Please Stop Gossiping" plank together. They can decorate it and paint it and make designing it a communal activity like fraternities with their paddles. Then, at the start of each prayer circle, just lay the "Please Stop Gossiping" plank in the middle of the room. The moment someone starts down that path, the first person to grab the plank gets to hit them. And the offender can't act surprised— because they helped design the plank. If they act indignant, just bust out the "splinter in my eye, plank upside yo' head" verse. That's in the Bible, and when the room stops spinning from the donnybrook you just initiated, you can show them the verse.

The plank is effective, but if you don't have access to wood, the fastest, easiest way to punch prayer gossip in the mouth— besides actually punching someone

FATHER, WE WANT TO LIFT UP BEFORE YOU ANDY AND MANDY, WHO WERE SEEN ███████ING WITH ███████, AND THEN THEY ███████ IN A ███████ ALL WEEKEND LONG.

in the mouth—is to say, "This is about you—isn't it?" Just insist that the horrible things your friend is gossiping about are actually true of them instead of somebody else. Keep saying, "This is about you—isn't it? Come on ... 'I have a friend named "Frank" who met a girl online in the Niagara Falls area and she stole his identity'? That's you, right? Someone stole your Social Security card and they're living it up, looking at big waterfalls and spending your cash." Eventually your gossiping friend will grow tired of your shenanigans and say something like, "Stop! It's not about me! I would never do something like that. That's horrible!" At which point you can say, "Aha! You're right. Those are horrible things, and you're telling us horrible things about your friends. In Proverbs 6:17–19, on the list of things God hates, gossip is listed with murder. Murder! What's next? Are you going to kill one of us? You are. Aren't you? A pox on you and your kin."

All right, you should probably leave out that last line about the pox. It's not particularly compassionate, and I probably just threw it in there because I wanted to make it seem like I read Shakespeare so much that sometimes it just spills out uncontrollably.

THE HEDGE OF PROTECTION: SLOW GROWING, EASILY JUMPED, NOT NEARLY ENOUGH PROTECTION FOR THESE CRAZY TIMES

I think the uber-popular Christian prayer request for a "hedge of protection" is in the Bible, but I'm not sure. It sounds like something David would have written in the book of Psalms. He's very poetic and our most Bono-like writer. But a friend of mine once revealed that he's always found that to be an inadequate security measure. As a child, when his mother would pray that he would have a hedge of protection or a hedge of angels around him, he would think, "Anyone can jump a hedge. How hard is that? Forget the hedge of angels; I'm praying for a dome of angels."

At first I laughed at that story, but the more I thought about it, the more it made sense. These are troubling times, and I've never seen a hedge and thought, "That thick collection of bushes is both terrifying and impenetrable." Maybe instead of praying for a hedge of protection, we should pray for:

A Beaded Curtain of Wasps

Your enemy would see this from a distance and think it was a standard beaded curtain. "Sweet," they'd think. "Hippies. Let's go steal their stuff." But as soon as they touched the curtain, they'd be rained down on by wasps that were enraged at being delicately strung together in a beaded curtain formation.

A Trampoline Moat of Lions

Throwing a plank across the average moat renders it useless. That won't be an issue though ... with the trampoline moat of lions, or T-MOL. You've admittedly got to pull insane permits to build this thing. But once you do, trust me, it's worth it. Few things are as scary and imposing as a pride of lions that have figured out the mechanics of a trampoline. Just imagine a hurricane of claws and fangs and manes bouncing skyward as they "give each other air." I'm getting sweaty just typing this.

A Rugby Scrum of Angels

When people say "a hedge of protection" or "a hedge of angels," I start imagining a bunch of angels in pleated khakis standing around, bored, waiting for the bus. Forget that. A rugby scrum is where players from both teams lock arms and heads and start swirling around in a tangle of power and aggression and swagger.

That's what I want angels protecting me to be doing. I want them to be constantly brawling, like some sort of angelic version of the Patrick Swayze movie *Roadhouse*. When something bad comes my way, the angels don't have to warm up. They just turn to my foe and say, "You want to get in on this? We got more than enough to go around."

LOVE ON

"You don't have to have sex on your wedding night. Be gentle." That's what an elderly friend of the family told me minutes after I tied the knot. Well me, and the guy filming the video, and anyone who ever watched the video.

MISSIONARY DATING: WHEN GOD CALLS YOU TO CONVERT THE SEXY AND UNCHURCHED

Sometimes the mission field God calls you to is hot, single people. It's rare, but it happens. You're just minding your own business, content in your own spiritual walk, when God will tap you on the shoulder and say, "I want you to reach the lost in local nightclubs and other singles hot spots. Please go out and date people into a relationship with me. I've seen the traffic numbers on eHarmony.com, and the harvest is indeed full."

That's a pretty sweet gig if you can get it. You get to go out to dinner a lot and see movies, which certainly beats slumming it in some third world country mission field. Sure, you've got to come up with creative excuses when your friends at church ask you, "Is that guy you're falling in love with a Christian?" But what do they know? This is different. You're different. They didn't receive the same call you did.

And besides, don't those naysayers know that marriage will change him? Marriage changes everything. I don't know the exact numbers, but I'm pretty sure 80 percent of guys who aren't Christian become so when you light a unity candle and read 1 Corinthians 13:4–6 at your wedding. If that doesn't work, then having a kid together will probably fix everything.

LOVE OFFERINGS

A love offering is kind of a "volunteer offering" the church takes up during special occasions, like when a puppet group from Guam (named "Strings of Mercy") is performing at your church. It's really not that voluntary though, because if you don't contribute anything, you're essentially telling everyone that your heart is not full of love. By not putting a couple of bucks in the offering plate, you're actually putting in a big fistful of hate.

I wish when the ushers collected a love offering they would say out loud when someone didn't give, "Oh, you don't have any love for the magical world of puppetry? I guess 'love your neighbor' doesn't include puppeteers? Fine, be that way."

TELLING OTHER PEOPLE MAYBE GOD GAVE THEM THE GIFT OF SINGLENESS

He didn't give it to me. I'm married, thank God, which I can totally say in this context because I am literally thanking God for something he gave me, which is a wife. It's weird that he didn't give you one though. Maybe he does want you to be lonely, I mean single. Like Paul. Marriage isn't for everyone. Not everyone gets that gift. Some people, yourself for instance, get cats instead.

Or dogs. God seems like he's more of a dog kind of guy. And that's not so bad. Dogs are nice, you'll have a lot of time by yourself for puzzles, and your tea will last twice as long. Think about that. Whenever my wife and I have tea we waste two teabags. Think of the savings in tea you'll be enjoying, and you'll never have to pick a side of the bed to sleep on. You have both sides to choose from and no one ever elbows you.

I bet you didn't even consider that. Good thing I'm so insightful, which is another gift God gave me. He gave me more of a "spiritual gift basket" than just an individual gift. I got marriage and happiness and kids and joy and love, but you got the gift of singleness. Like Paul. That's great. Seriously, I'll pray you'll be willing to embrace it and not shriek every morning when you awake and that gift is still sitting on your doorstep. That's what I would do. I have nightmares about being alone sometimes. But that's your gift.

ABSTINENCE

I'm a huge fan of abstinence. Especially now that I'm married and don't have to practice it. But I almost didn't write about it because I think that despite how much we like the *idea* of abstinence, we've done a really poor job explaining its benefits. Here's what usually happens for thirteen-year-old Christian boys:

Their parents or their youth leader says, "Look, you should stay pure and not have sex so that you can keep your marriage holy." That's their first option.

Then the world says to them, "Look at me! Sex is wild and fun and neon and loud and Whoa! Spring Break! Party!"

As a thirteen-year-old, it was unfortunately pretty easy to decide which idea sounded more interesting.

What if instead, we told people that a great reason to wait until marriage to have sex is that it makes your sex life so much better after you're married? When you don't bring baggage into the sexual aspect of your marriage relationship, things get wild a lot faster. You get to have crazy, awesome, Prince-type sex. There are no memories of other people, no hang-ups to work through. It's just you and your wife getting ridiculous and enjoying the hot, sexy good time that holiness makes possible.

This is truly what it sounds like ... when doves cry.

FALLING IN LOVE ON A MISSION TRIP

My little brother wrote one of my favorite songs in the world while he was on a mission trip to Africa. It wasn't about the people. It wasn't about the culture. It was about something much bigger and more universally understood than that. It was about falling in love on a mission trip.

This happens a lot. We go away on a mission trip. We fall in love. We break up when we get back. Why does it happen? Why do we do this? I have a few ideas:

Your relationship back home doesn't stand a chance.

When you go on a mission trip and leave your boyfriend at home, you'll start to see Mark, that awkward but kind of cute guy on the trip, in a whole new light. It's a light called, "Look at Mark feed hungry children in Africa while my boyfriend plays Xbox back in Ohio." The person back home is instantly eclipsed. I don't care how great they are—they're not on the mission trip helping people. Caring about people, being a servant of the Lord in a tangible, visible way. Doing things that aren't selfish or self-centered. "And come to think of it, my boyfriend and I don't even like the same music. And I love that you like weird ethnic food too, and helping people. Can you hold on for a minute? I need to go see if there's a phone in this village. I have to break up with someone."

You get this weird common language with fellow mission trippers.

"Hey, remember that time when we all hiked up that little river in the jungle and there was that crazy orange lizard? And for the rest of the trip, we called anything that was crazy an 'orange-lizard situation'? That was hilarious. And then that time Frank said, 'Bring your Bobbles to church,' instead of, 'Bring your Bibles?' That was so funny! Nobody gets those stories like you. Let's fall in love on the last day of the trip and then break up when we get dropped off back at the church parking lot. I mission trip love you!"

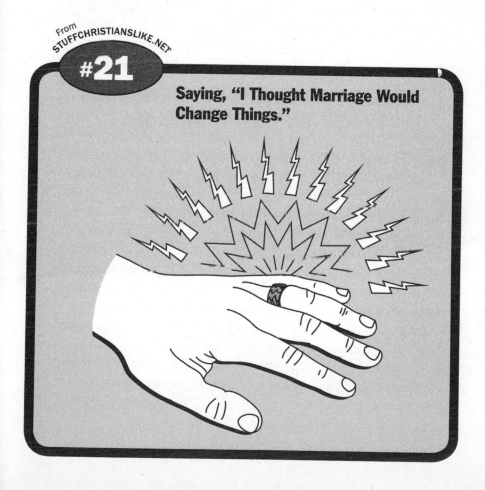

From STUFFCHRISTIANSLIKE.NET

#21

Saying, "I Thought Marriage Would Change Things."

You get to see the real person on a mission trip.

Anyone can be nice and polite on a date to Chili's. Anyone can open your car door and slide your chair out before you both eat baby back, baby back ribs. But when it's 100 degrees in the shade, and you're sweaty and dirty, and you have to perform one more Noah's ark puppet show for kids in a desert, you're going to be real. And seeing how someone really is, who they are in the tough situations and the easy situations, is a pretty intoxicating thing.

If your girlfriend goes on a mission trip without you and immediately tells you "we need to talk" upon getting back, don't say I didn't warn you.

Go on that trip. Always go on that trip.

MAKING SURE EVERYONE KNOWS YOUR FIANCÉ ISN'T LIVING WITH YOU

Want to torture a Christian who recently got engaged? Don't allow them any space in the conversation to tell you that they're not living with their fiancé. That's some good fun, my friend, because we want to tell you that. We want to be up front that we're not living in sin, that we're not co-habiting, and we'll do *anything* to work that into the flow of the discussion. But we don't want to say "living in sin" because it kind of makes us sound like we're weirdo Christians, so we'll go to great creative lengths to tell you that we have two separate residences:

"We're really excited to be getting married. It'll be nice not to pay two mortgages when we tie the knot."

"I cooked dinner for my fiancé last night at my place, but I was out of salt, so he drove to his place, in a car, because the distance is significant."

"She has a cat, and I've never lived with a cat, so when we get married and both she and the cat move in, that will be a change."

"My fiancée's apartment flooded. So she stayed at my place, while I slept on the couch, in the living room of the apartment I share with a roommate. Who was there the whole time and actually kept a sleepless vigil in the hall."

"I'm engaged to a girl who lives across town. Lives clear across town without any sort of tunnels or skywalks that connect our two houses. Completely separate."

I personally never got caught up in the fancy ways to say "we're not living in sin." I was living in a trailer home in a retirement community when I was engaged, and there was very little chance the community would have stood for any of that shacking up nonsense.

Sure, while living there I mentally aged about forty years in a matter of weeks, sitting in a rocking chair with a quilt over my knees and a foot massager I requested for Christmas because they were all the rage in my new old neighborhood. I may have suddenly fallen in love with *Everybody Loves Raymond* and chuckled at that rascal's antics like an old man, but other than that, everything worked out.

My wife didn't become old. She lived across town with the Morrisons. In their house. Which was different from a trailer park. Where I slept. Alone by myself.

GETTING CAUGHT OFF GUARD BY DIVORCE

I'm married and if you are too, then statistically speaking, one of us is getting divorced.

"Hold up one second!" you might say. "That can't be true. I'm a Christian. I've seen studies that indicate that Christians actually have a lower divorce rate, something like 33 percent instead of a 50 percent divorce rate like the rest of the country. How dare you misinform me!"

Shame on me, but arguing about whether Christians have a 33 percent or a 50 percent divorce rate is ridiculous. Look at it this way: Would it make a huge difference if one out of every three neighbors on your street got mauled to death by a bear or one out of every two? Would you sit around with friends and say, "Those bear stats are grossly exaggerated. I read that there are only 33 deadly Grizzly bears in our gated community, not 50. The media is so biased!"

No, regardless of the statistic, you'd be more careful about bears. You'd buy books on how to keep your house safe from bears. You'd carry a gun and bear spray. And when Valentine's Day rolled around, you'd probably buy your wife a hot water heater.

Okay, one of those sentences had nothing to do with the metaphor but was in fact true. In my defense, it was a "State Select" model, which I've been assured is one of the sexier hot water heaters available. So don't worry about us becoming a statistic; we'll be fine.

CHURCH

If church is about worshipping God and not about me, then why did I break into a cold sweat when my wife started knitting one Sunday as we waited for service to start?

"What are you doing? Put that away," I said in a hushed whisper.

"What? I'm just knitting. What's the big deal?" my wife said, clearly startled at my shallowness.

The big deal was that I mistakenly thought knitting was for almost-dead people. At the time I didn't realize how hip and artistic knitting really was. I thought it was for old people who called the internet the "World Wide Interwebs" and collected plates commemorating events. It's bad enough people near us don't know we direct deposit our tithe and have a perfectly legitimate reason to stiff the offering bucket. Now I felt like I might as well be whittling a pipe out of a corn cob or churning fresh butter.

THE METROSEXUAL WORSHIP LEADER

When you tell someone about your church, there's unfortunately not a standard system to describe the degree of metrosexuality your worship leader possesses. Wouldn't it be awesome to say, "You'll love my church and the music. We have a 78-point metrosexual worship leader"? Or if you were driving by a church and you saw a hip-looking "42" in the corner of the sign, you'd know instantly how metro the worship experience was going to be.

Doesn't that sound fantastic? I think so, and as a service to churches around the world, I created an easy rating system to analyze how metrosexual your worship leader is:

Metrosexual Worship Leader Scorecard

1. Has a faux hawk hairstyle .... +1
2. Has more product in his hair than your wife .... +1
3. Has Rob Bell-style, black-rimmed glasses .... +1
4. They are not prescription, but just for effect..... +2
5. Attends the Catalyst Conference .... +3
6. Performs at the Catalyst Conference .... +10
7. Owns white Puma, Vans, Asics,
   or Diesel sneakers .... +2 for each pair
8. Wears jeans on stage............................... +1
9. Wears designer jeans on stage .... +2
10. Wears designer ladies jeans on stage .... +4
11. Wears Wrangler or Rustler jeans on stage .... -3
12. Has a goatee....................................... +2
13. Wears one of those Castro revolution looking hats .... +2
14. Drinks coffee on stage .... +1
15. Drinks some kind of coffee you did not
    know existed..................................... +2
16. Brings a French press on stage and makes
    his own coffee during service .... +5
17. Has a handlebar mustache........................... -3
18. Good at Frisbee but hates getting all "sweaty" ......+1
19. Has a haircut that covers one of his eyes
    while singing.................................... +1

20. Owns a white belt .... +2
21. Wears suspenders, although not in an ironic way ..... -3
22. Wears a scarf with a T-shirt .... +1
23. Wears a winter knit hat even in the summer .... +2
24. Reads quotes from the Bible between songs
    using his iPhone or Kindle .... +3
25. Drives an Audi or VW (silver, of course) .... +2
26. Uses the words *postmodern*, *relevant*, or
    emergent nonstop .... +2
27. Cringes a little when people say the
    "H word" (Hymnal) .... +3
28. Owns a Grizzly Adams red and black
    flannel shirt .... -2
29. Named his kid after a color, number, or city .... +2
30. Casually references Norwegian punk bands
    you've never heard of .... +2
31. Wears a tie .... -1
32. Wears a tie as a belt .... +2
33. Looks as if he might exfoliate .... +2
34. Has a man bag or European Carry-All .... +2
35. Brings said bag onstage with him .... +3
36. Has a tattoo .... +2
37. Has a visible tattoo .... +4
38. Wife accompanies him on stage and plays
    tambourine .... -4
39. Was formerly in a punk new wave band .... +2
40. Is currently in a punk new wave band .... +3
41. Your wife ever says, "He needs a barrette
    for his hair." .... +2
42. Has a soul patch .... +3
43. Won't play barefoot on stage until he gets
    a pedicure .... +2
44. Refers to California as "the left coast" .... +2
45. Twitters and updates his blog while
    leading worship .... +2
46. Read that last line and laughed at how outdated
    Twitter is because he's already using some sort
    of hologram technology the rest of the world
    won't find out about for three years .... +4
47. His toddler dresses cooler than you .... +2

How did your worship leader score? How did you score? And what's it all mean? I'm glad you asked. Here's how to assess a point total:

1–10 points = Hymnal Hero

You, my friend, are what is known in the industry as a "Hymnal Hero." (That's the industry of sarcasm, by the way.) You're not metro in the least bit. You don't like fruit-flavored Chapstick and think that songs that were written in this century, or the last one for that matter, are "too new." If married, your wife tries to get you to wear hip jeans, but you're not into it. When my cologne that smells like old hymnals comes out, you will buy a case.

11–20 points = Tomlin Curious

Oh, well hello there, you're Tomlin Curious. I am, of course, referring to Chris Tomlin, one of the founding fathers of metrosexual worship leading. You're currently dipping a toe, possibly even a pedicured toe, into the idea of all this. You still rock the occasional hymn, but recently you saw a wide leather bracelet at the mall and thought about getting it. When you sleep at night, you can hear voices calling you, "Come style your hair . . . Come frost your tips."

21–40 points = Goatee Guy

Right now, you're wearing Pumas and drinking a coffee that has fourteen words in its name. It's cool—I have Pumas on too. You've gone over to the salmon side. (This is the side where instead of saying "pink," you say things are "salmon" or "melon" or "coral.") You rarely play a hymn and style yourself after Jeremy Camp. For breakfast you had something with "wheatgrass" in it.

41+ points = Girl Jeans Gambler

I've never personally rocked the girls' jeans because they make my legs look really skinny. Oh, and also I'm a boy. But you're thinking about it. You might not be ready to do the eyeliner thing, but when you shop for clothes, you get a little tempted to hit up the makeup counter. You've never sung a hymn and think Chris Tomlin is "too traditional."

Copious amounts of "product" creating a faux hawk or "on purpose bed head."

Voluminous winter scarf regardless that it's 100 degrees outside

Complicated coffee with 37 first names. Will be held when not quoting Bible verses directly from his iPhone.

Bedazzled, embellished, fantastical jeans that glimmer like a unicorn's mane when he moves.

Canvas shoes that look to cost about $2 but were actually the same price as a monthly payment on his car (Silver Audi or VW).

Architectural stool best paired with the small, hip table minister will use during sermon.

0 = Metrotastical

Surprisingly enough, zero is the highest degree of metrosexuality you can possess. Why? Because it's a trend and trends change. So if you're truly a metrosexual worship leader of the highest degree, by the time this book comes out, you will have moved on to what's next, which will probably be homemade clothing. You'll be knitting your own oddly shaped jeans and chunky socks on stage in between songs. And I'll be in the crowd finally wearing a white belt and saying, "Come on! Now I have to learn how to knit to stay cool? You guys are killing me."

TUNING OUT IF THE MINISTER IS YOUNGER THAN YOU

Sure Whitney Houston, I believe that children are the future, but I'd be lying if I said that's the first thing I think when a minister younger than me takes the stage. Call it jealousy that the next generation is about to lap me or that the generation behind me has a cooler name, "millennial tweener x-tremes," but when youth is served at church, sometimes Christians like to tune out and think:

"Oh no, where's the regular pastor? Is it 'regular' or 'senior' or 'teaching pastor of imaginevisioneering'? I can never get those right, but who is this kid up on stage? Is he doing the announcements? Is there a youth group fundraiser I need to know about? Fine, I'll get my car washed in a Chick-fil-A parking lot. That's like a win-win right there, holding a Christian event in the parking lot of a Christian restaurant. That's God squared.

But why isn't this kid getting off the stage? Is he, no, is he about to preach? Is it youth Sunday already? What, he's the youth minister? That's great, but this isn't youth group. He's way too young to school me in the game of life. Oh, but this is happening. It's too late for me to walk out and leave. It's time for the junior hour of power.

Please just don't use that phrase that all young ministers bust out. Please don't say, oh no, you just did. You just said, "When I was growing up."

You said it like it was over, like you've crossed from young man into wizened old gentleman. But you're only twenty-four. The toughest decision you've faced in life so far was whether to get the full meal plan or the five-day-a-week meal plan at seminary. You went with the five? That's good to know, let me scribble that down here in the sermon notes section of my bulletin.

But I'll forgive you that one. I'll let that one slide as long as you don't give me any marital advice. You've been married for about fifteen minutes. You're still tan from your honeymoon. I can still kind of smell suntan lotion on you. If at any point in this sermon you try to give me marriage advice, I am going to think about college basketball. I just want to be up front about that. The toughest marriage decision you've faced so far is whether to exchange one of the china sets you got as a wedding gift for a George Foreman grill that is shaped like a massive charcoal grill. Don't. I've done that, I fought that battle, and it was not worth it. You need more plates than you think and less George Foreman grills than you think. Trust me on that.

See, I should be doing this sermon, I just gave you some free marital advice. You're welcome.

CROCK-POTS, A LOVE LETTER

Dear Crock-Pot,

Is there anything your circle of goodness can't deliver?

Any bounty of deliciousness you are incapable of providing?

Any warm embrace of bubbly food delightfulness you are unwilling to share?

I say no, but you don't come around as often as you used to. We're all trying to live a little healthier. We're eating fewer dishes that look

like macaroni, cheese, and beef got into a street
fight. When I go to potlucks, I can't find you among
the plates of organically grown seaweed burgers.
I look—oh, I promise you I look—but you remain
elusive. No miniature hot dogs swimming in mysterious
red sauce, no unidentifiable stew that is the color
of Burnt Sienna crayons. Somewhere you sit alone in
a cabinet, instead of in your rightful place of honor.

You're so forgiving, too. We can just throw
something in you and completely forget about
cooking all day. Even if that meal spends an hour
too long in your hot belly, it's okay. You won't burn
it. You won't hurt it. Your love is tender. You always
give, you never take away.

If there were a Dish Hall of Fame, I would
nominate you. If there were an NCAA-type
tournament for cookware, I would pick you to win
my bracket. If Mount Rushmore had room for an
additional American hero, your rotund face would
sing from the mountains.

I love you, Crock-Pot.

Forever yours,
Jonathan

RAISING OUR HANDS IN WORSHIP

Christians like to sing with their hands raised. I know this
because I watch them. In church I am constantly studying the
different styles of arm extensions. (Insert a "Worship is about
God, not watching other people" judgmental statement right
about here.) And in my many, many years between the aisles,
here are the five different hand-raising styles I have noticed
most often:

The Ninja

You are tricky, sir, truly tricky. The Ninja is testing the waters. He sees ladies fling their arms into the air at the first note of a praise song, but he's not so sure. What if his friends see him? He used to make fun of people who did that. So instead of going all out, he does a fancy little move. He puts his hands by his pants pockets with the palms facing the heavens. From behind, you can't see that he's doing anything out of the ordinary. From the front it just looks like he's cupping his hands slightly, as if displaying the contents of his pockets.

The Half & Half

This person often wants to sing with both hands raised, but they attend a conservative church and don't want to be known as "that guy." Instead, they hold one in the air, placing the other one in their pocket or on the chair in front of them. It's like half their body is screaming, "YAY, JESUS!" and the other half is whispering, "Nothing to see here, folks. Move it along, please ... move it along."

The Pound Cake

This is what we in the industry refer to as an "underhand move." Instead of reaching your arms upward, you hold them slightly in front of you, palms turned toward the sky, as if expecting to receive something from someone in front of you. The Pound Cake places your elbows at stomach level, your hands tilted at a 47-degree angle, as if someone visiting your housewarming party is about to hand you a delicious pound cake. It's not a heavy cake, so you don't have to brace yourself. Instead, you just relax and think, "Hey, cool. Pound cake. Let me take that for you."

47-degree angle

The Double High Five

I'm stingy with my high fives. I think the last time I gave one was in the delivery room of my second daughter. The next time I give one will be if this book sells more than nineteen copies. Other than those two situations, I find the high five to be the physical equivalent of using a lot of exclamation marks!!! That's why I rarely do this move. The double high five looks exactly like it sounds. You act like you've just scored a touchdown and are about to double high five the person in front of you. (Some people call this move the "Secret Passageway" because it kind of looks like you are feeling along a wall for a hidden button that will open a secret door. But I'm a purist and don't use that term.)

The YMCA

This is my favorite, and probably the most common hand raising technique. It's not complicated and regularly makes cameos in magazine ads for Christian colleges. Much like the famous song, you simply raise your hands above your body and form a big Y. That's all. But it leaves little doubt to the folks around you about what's going on. You're worshipping. It's big, it's beautiful, it's messy, and it's great. A friend of mine said that when her mom did it, it always looked like she was clearing a runway for God to land.

I tend to be a Ninja guy myself.

FEARING YOUR CHURCH WILL DO SOMETHING WACKY THE ONE TIME YOU INVITE A FRIEND

The only thing Christians like more than inviting friends, co-workers, and family members to church is fearing that on the

Sunday they do, all hell will break loose during service. (Not a swear. This is a Christian book; I get to use that one.)

It doesn't matter how great your church is Sunday after Sunday. On the one day you actually invite a neighbor for the first time, there's a moment of panic that passes through you.

Worship music top notch week after week? Well this will be the Sunday the lady who owns a mission trip rain stick souvenir will be doing an interpretation of the song "I Can Only Imagine."

Pastor always brings his A game? Well this will be the Sunday he starts his sermon by saying, "Today I want to talk about why you should give all your money to the church unless you want to go to hell."

Never done any old school snake handling at your church? Well this will be the Sunday where they hand out a free pit viper with each bulletin.

Your only defense against this fear is to prepare a really good church disclaimer. As soon as the service jumps off the tracks and you see your friend squirm, lean over to them and call a mulligan, "Church is never like this. I don't know what's going on today. Will you please come back next week?"

PRETENDING YOU'RE NOT CRYING DURING CHURCH

I cried once at a Fuddruckers hamburger restaurant during lunch. No, it wasn't the time I participated in a two-pound cheeseburger eating contest and got the meat sweats while throwing up that afternoon in my cubicle at work. It was just a normal lunch with a guy from the office. We started talking about how crazy God's love is and before I knew it, I was tearing up right there over a plate of onion rings.

I don't know why guys can't cry at church, but it's a law. Fortunately, there are a few ways to pretend you're not crying:

Sniff, don't sniffle.

There's a huge difference. A sniff is what a man does when he has a cold. A tough, manly cold. A sniffle is what a small puppy does when it's crying in church. Pretend you have a cold. If you think you're going to cry, fake sneeze a few times, blow your nose into a tissue, and mutter to the people around you, "This darn cold! Got it ice fishing … for sharks … with my bare hands."

Look up as if condensation has fallen on your face from the ceiling.

Best-case scenario is that you keep the tears in your orbital region and never allow them to escape your eye. But let's say one makes a break for your cheek. When you feel that wet renegade creeping down, immediately look up at the ceiling. I don't care if it's 12 feet away or 100 feet away—react as if condensation from the air conditioner has just dripped on your rugged, masculine cheek. Then proceed to punch that little pool of water off your face. Stupid ceiling leak.

Never use the back of your hand.

You know who wipes their tears with the back of their hands? People who've just finished watching a Lifetime Channel movie called *Stolen Innocence*, where the heroine had her heart broken by a horrible man and lost everything she had but in losing her way found herself and the will to survive. That's who uses the back of their hand to wipe tears. Not you. You use the tips of your thumb and your pointer finger. Put one on each side of your nose and make clockwise circles as if you are rubbing the tension out of your face from wearing glasses for too long. You'll look pensive and maybe even thoughtful, like you're trying to concentrate. All the while you'll secretly be wiping away tears. Works like a charm.

There are more tips, but most are pretty complicated and involve props like pirate eye patches and smoke bombs. You'll probably want to stick with these. If you can't—if you end up crying in the middle of church—counteract that wanton show of emotion by volunteering to tear down the band equipment or stack up all the chairs in the sanctuary. Alone. Wearing a red and black flannel shirt like a lumberjack. That'll fix 'em; that'll fix 'em good.

ALTAR CALLS

An altar call is when the pastor encourages you to come down front and give your life to Jesus. Those are pretty straightforward events. You go down, you pray a prayer with someone (usually on staff), you go home. Not that giving your life to Jesus is straightforward—please save the hate mail—but the altar call is pretty cut and dried.

Where it starts getting weird is when the minister invites people to come down and pray at the front of the church. In a moment of odd "no rules, no worries" pastor behavior, he'll say, "We're going to invite you to come up here and pray if you feel led. If you feel like there's something you need to give to Jesus or that God is pushing on you, come down to the front. We'll sing another song and give you time to get right with God."

One Sunday morning, that happened to me at church. The thought of walking down the aisle In front of 5,000 people wasn't that appealing, but when God gives me the "it's go time" tap, I usually respond. I leaned over to my wife and said, "Uh oh, I think I'm supposed to go down." She leaned back over and said, "I love you, but I'm not going." I told her, "I'll pray for your heathen soul and ask that someday you'll have the deep faith I currently possess." Then I went down. Overall, it was a great experience, but there are some things I wish I had remembered before I headed to the front:

Don't assume your friends are going to go down with you.

I know this is dumb, but when I went forward, it also happened to be the first time we'd ever sat with our friends Ben and Sheila. When the minister said you should "take a friend down to the front with you," I automatically gave God an extra high five for getting Ben and Sheila to sit with us. I didn't head-nod to Ben or ask him to come down, I just figured he'd naturally follow me out like Billy Zane followed Tom Berenger in the movie *Sniper*. That didn't happen. I thought maybe he was praying in his seat and was going to come up and place his hand on my back in a few minutes like some sort of Christian Cavalry.

Don't excuse yourself down the row by saying, "Pardon me, sinner ... I'm answering the call of God."

It's not a race. There's plenty of "front-of-the-church Holy Spirit" to go around for everyone. If fighting with someone in the church parking lot is bad, just imagine how much God hates when you shove people on the way to his altar. Or maybe he doesn't like people who mosey when you're trying to sprint to where he called you. I could really go both ways on that one.

Don't get frustrated that you didn't get a "good prayer spot."

If you're behind someone slow on your walk up front, chances are you're going to get a bad spot to pray. You'll probably be off to the side by the stairs, which is the prayer equivalent of being seated by the kitchen at a restaurant. Or you'll be kneeling on painful power cords for some instrument. It's horrible for you to even think these things, but you're going to and that's okay.

Don't expect superpowers afterward.

I wasn't able to fly after I went down front that Sunday. I was kind of hoping that I'd be able to move things with my mind, or maybe jump a little higher, or at the bare minimum, be an inch taller. Didn't happen. In fact, I think later that day I was a jerk to my wife.

On the Jonathan scale, the whole thing was kind of a bust. Ben didn't come down. I didn't get a good prayer spot. God didn't zap me. Fortunately, going down front isn't measured according to my standards.

From
STUFFCHRISTIANSLIKE.NET

#187

Leaving Room for the Holy Spirit When You Dance.

When in doubt, stay at least one Bible length away.

Christian rock.

Insert Holy Spirit here.

USING VACATION BIBLE SCHOOL AS FREE BABYSITTING

Denomination, schomenation, when our kids are out of school for the summer and we've suddenly got to fill eight weeks of time with activities, we Christians like to put aside our denominational differences and bounce our kids like Ping-Pong balls around the county to different Vacation Bible School programs.

We sent our kids to three different churches last summer, in part because our church refuses to hold Vacation Bible School. One day, my daughter L.E. came home from one of the more "rural" churches we had selected for our "tour de VBS," and I asked her what she learned that day. Her response?

"We watched *The Little Mermaid* movie."

Hmm, I thought to myself, I'm not sure which part of the Bible Disney is taking that story from, but I've got to work all week and God did make the ocean after all and in a way, that movie is kind of similar to the Jonah story.

"Have a good time tomorrow, sweetheart."

THE COOL YOUTH GROUP ROOM

If I ever start my own church, iGracePointeLifeTruthHouse-NorthRiverElevate, I won't need to hire a youth minister. I like them. I have nothing against goatees or Frisbee, it's not that. It's just that I won't need a youth minister. I've got outreach taken care of already. I have a foolproof plan on how to connect with every teenager in our community—a cool youth group room.

Seriously, why would I hire a full-time youth minister when I can get a real working traffic light for only $378? Have you ever seen those in action? You put one of those in the corner of your youth room, maybe pair it with a STOP sign and a mural of an open road or somebody smashing through a wall, and you're going to break fire codes with the amount of kids that come to youth group.

I can just hear kids I-M-ing about it on the internets right now:

> TEEN 1: Let's go to that new church in town.
> TEEN 2: Y? (That means "why." These kids today with their abbreviations! It's wacky!)
> TEEN 1: They have a room called "the hangout spot" and there's a traffic light in the corner.
> TEEN 2: Wait, a real working traffic light? Like the kind that I would see in the street? Get out of here.
> TEEN 1: Seriously. And they have a booth in this other corner; it's like a coffee shop. They call that corner "the café."
> TEEN 2: A real booth? Oh man, if you tell me they have a mural, I am going to flip my lid. (Kids these days are always flipping their lids. You gotta stay on top of this phresh language.)
> TEEN 1: Let's go!

You're thinking about coming right now, aren't you, and I didn't even tell you about the section of bleachers we put in there and the fog machine. Sorry though, unless you're a "tweener" you can't come hang out at "Projekt Xcitement." Feel free to attend our Single's Ministry though, where we'll try to help cure you of your singleness.

FINDING TYPOS IN THE WORSHIP MUSIC

I'm a professional copywriter. I am, in theory, supposed to be a highly honed, detail-dedicated arbiter of punctuation and grammar. That's why I look for typos in the worship songs at church. What's your excuse?

I know, I know ... you didn't mean to. It was just up there on the screen, letters that are two feet tall practically screaming out at you, "Look at me, I'm a typo! Who's got two J's in their name and is here to love you in the chorus of this song? His name is JJesus!"

And then you're stuck. It only takes one hit to become an addict. You want to stop. Deep down inside, you know you're supposed to be worshipping, to be communing with the Holy Spirit in song and praise, but now it's too late. After that first typo, you start noticing more. And if the words are all spelled correctly, you start picking up on spacing problems. That "Thank you" should have been on the same line as "Jesus," you think to yourself. That "Jesus" is just a widow down there, all alone on its own line. Poor little lonely Jesus, stuck down in a corner of the screen by himself.

Nobody puts Jesus in a corner. Oh great, now you're thinking about lines from the movie *Dirty Dancing* during the middle of the sermon. And you're mad that you have to stand during worship because it's hard to write down the number of mistakes you found in the bulletin unless you're sitting.

Now you're proofreading the bulletin, which isn't really fair, because the person who put that together probably had about thirteen seconds to get it to the printer, and the bake sale folks were late getting their info in, so is it her fault there's a "Cank Sale" this Sunday? That kind of sounds like the abbreviation for *cankle*, which is when your legs just go right into your feet with no discernible ankle, you think to yourself. You've got to be kidding me. Now you're judging people's body images? Everyone else is singing "Blessed Be Your Name," and you're judging the cankles of the people in the row next to you?

#408

The Double Greeting

THE "GOOD MORNING" FLOW CHART

Say "Good morning."

Does the congregation respond?

YES → Is their response loud enough to damage their own hearing?

YES →

NO ↓

Repeat the greeting, shaming the crowd by comparing them to a louder, more in love with God, crowd.

NO ↓

Repeat, louder this time: **"I SAID, 'GOOD MORNING!'"**

Does the congregation respond *now*?

YES →

NO ↓

Acknowledge your approval. Proceed with morning worship.

Have you done this six times already?

YES → Shake head sadly. Proceed with morning worship.

NO ↓

MINISTERS! CLIP OUT THIS PAGE AND USE IT NEXT SUNDAY MORNING!

REPORTING TO THE PASTOR IN EXQUISITE DETAIL EVERYTHING BAD HIS SON HAS BEEN UP TO SO THAT WHEN HIS SON FINALLY DOES CONFESS TO KISSING THAT GIRL AT CHURCH, MY DAD REPLIES, "I ALREADY KNOW; THE DEACONS TOLD ME."

Thanks.

LOSING THE WILL TO CLAP DURING SONGS

I always cringe a little when a worship leader says, "Everybody clap together" at the beginning of a song.

Instead of marching forward in a united rhythm, what usually happens in church sounds like someone lit off a box of hand firecrackers. Smacks and slaps and claps just ringing out randomly with no sense of where the song is headed. After years of witnessing claps die merciless deaths at church, I thought it might be good to analyze how the clap goes so wrong, so quickly. Here's what I think happens, laid out in a convenient chronological explanation:

Step 1. We get the "call to arms."

The worship leader tells everyone in the crowd to start clapping. Often, he raises his hands above his head to demonstrate. It's an exciting moment. The world is fresh and new. We're all a little intoxicated on the sense of potential and possibility. So together, we start clapping.

Step 2. We realize there's no leader.

Eventually, the worship leader stops clapping above his head. Either he starts playing an instrument or grabs his microphone in a dramatic, Creed-like moment. Suddenly, we in the crowd realize no one is leading this clap-a-thon. We're all alone. We scan the stage for direction, but no one bails us out. The main singer is focused on the song, and the backup singers are doing some sort of PhD-level, rhythmic clapping that's beyond us. At least 15 percent of people call it quits right here.

Step 3. We'll give you the first verse and that's it.

Most people feel pretty generous if they clap for the entire first verse. We won't go the whole song, but at least we pitched in. It's the equivalent of serving at church by stacking chairs. You still feel like you gave something back to the church, but you didn't have to interact with anyone or get up early. About 40 percent of people quit clapping here.

Step 4: We find out the chorus is faster.

Whoa, whoa, whoa! Just when some of us have decided to keep clapping, we run into a chorus that defies all logic. It's suddenly faster than the verse was and we don't know what to do. Do we speed up our clapping? Do we stop and pick back up on the second verse? Somebody, please, a little help! More than 20 percent of people quit here.

Step 5: We finish the song.

At last this crazy ride is over, the clapping is done. We're finished and can feel good about what we've accomplished. But just know this: If you ask us to clap on a second song, about 50 percent of us will flat-out refuse. We're all clapped out.

THE CASSEROLE OF HOPE

A casserole of hope is a food dish that a Christian gives you after a tragedy. It usually involves pasta and cheese in some format, but sometimes, if they really love you, they'll make something in a crock pot. The challenge, though, is that it's hard to know what to give someone. Do you make something big and hearty or light and fruity? Is it one meal or a series of meals? Is a dessert too frivolous? Does a serious situation require a serious meal, like some sort of melodramatic stew?

Fortunately, I've come up with an easy list of what types of dishes certain tragedies require. Tear it out and put it on your fridge. It will serve you well in times of need and casserole.

Car wreck

This depends of course on the severity of the crash, but the key here is to give food that's not portable. Chances are the crash might have occurred when they tried to make a cell phone call while driving and eating a twenty-seven-layer burrito at the same time. Don't tempt them with any food that's in tube form or easy to eat in the car. Give them soup with a packet of forks. It's really hard to eat soup with a fork in a moving car.

Fire

Nothing baked. Nothing spicy. Nothing seared. Nothing grilled. The important thing is not to bring any food that will remind them of the fire. The last thing they'll want is your famous "four alarm chicken wings." Give them something carved of ice. I'm not sure what that is, but you can probably get one at Whole Foods.

Hole in bedroom ceiling made while chasing a squirrel

Beef jerky. For starters, the person whose ceiling was wrecked by a friend possibly named Jeff who was texting a girl instead of staying focused on the squirrel chase at hand can pretend the jerky is the squirrel. Also, jerky is portable in case this hypothetical person named Jonathan Acuff is required to take an overnight trip to the couch because he messed up his bedroom, which his wife completely didn't see the humor in. And lastly, the squirrel is still loose and your friend will need a meal he can eat on the run—or on the rafters of his attic, as it were.

Loss of employment

I don't know what to give someone who lost their job. But I know what *not* to get them: Easy Mac, those small, microwaveable packets of macaroni and cheese. When a company I worked for went out of business, I took what I called "the summer of Jon." (Or as my in-laws called it, "The summer of the guy who married our daughter, took her from Georgia to Boston, and promptly lost his job.") My wife's one rule was that I had to get up when she did for work. That meant that at 6:30 every morning, I was showered and dressed with nowhere to go. I decided to kill time by eating Easy Mac for breakfast and lunch and snacks. I gained about fifteen pounds. Give an unemployed person a salad.

Don't worry too much about nutrition when someone is going through a difficult time. If they wrecked their car or the house caught on fire, the last thing people are concerned about is exercising their "core" and getting enough lycopene.

CHURCH NAMES THAT SOUND LIKE DESIGNER CLOTHING STORES

My cousin attends a church called "Warehouse 242." There's another church in his area called "Elevation." In Durham, North Carolina, there's a church called, simply, "The Summit." I'm not sure when it happened, but at some point we started naming our churches after stores that sell designer jeans. And I'm cool with that. I don't think you have to name something the "Back to the Bible Holiness Church" — which is outside of Atlanta in case you want to attend.

I think it might even be a great thing to have a funky name because it opens up some good conversations with people. Imagine you're at work on Monday and someone says, "What'd you do this weekend?"

You can reply, "I hung out at Elevation."

Your friend will then say, "Is that the new salsa/techno/hip-hop/Southern Cambodian traditional dance club? I've heard the girls in that place are ridiculous."

At which point you can answer, "No, it's a church," and then proceed to share the entire gospel with him and possibly get him plugged into a small group on the spot.

Okay, it might not go down exactly that way, but at the bare minimum, saying you went to "Elevation" is going to at least keep the conversation rolling and possibly even raise some questions. If you said, "I went to 'God Is Awesome, Praise Jesus Cathedral of Hope and Light' over the weekend," your friend might throw a handful of glitter and climb out a window to escape the conversation. Which is never a good thing.

THE FAKE SERMON ILLUSTRATION

On a Monday morning right before a meeting at work, I got the following phone call from my three-year-old's preschool.

"Hi, Mr. Acuff. This is Susan at Small Wonder. McRae ate some sort of fungus on the playground. We've got Poison Control on the other line and have saved a sample of what she ate. They don't think it's going to be a problem, but we need to keep an eye on her for a few hours."

It turns out, there's a white, clumpy fungus that grows in bark mulch called "dog vomit fungus." While playing outside, McRae saw some and thought to herself, "Hey, free marshmal-lows!" and proceeded to eat as much as her little hands could grab. Then when they lined up the kids to bring them inside, the teachers saw McRae's fungus-covered face and asked, "Oh sweetheart, what have you been eating?" McRae, blessed with her father's heart of a servant, immediately answered, "I'll show you," and walked the teachers over to the bark mulch buffet she had been enjoying during recess.

That reminds me a lot of God.

Not really, but I wanted it to. I tried to think of a way to write something about sin and how it looks good at first but then if we eat it, we end up throwing up all night and sleeping on the floor in our parents' room. I looked and looked for a segue, but ultimately I realized that if I tried to connect that story to the Bible or God I would just be perpetuating a "fake sermon illustration."

A fake sermon illustration is when a pastor is desperate to tell a story but can't figure out a way to tie it back into his sermon. It's something funny that happened to him, something silly his kids did, or maybe even a movie clip that really shook him up emotionally. But he can't find the bridge between the illustration and the message, so he just tries to sneak it by you really fast and hope that you don't notice.

I prefer that the minister says one of two things instead:

"Now let's talk about God." I have a friend who can hear a story about low test scores in public high schools and then say, "That reminds me, I was thinking about eating sushi tonight." What he means when he says, "that reminds me," is not, "here's something related to what you're talking about." He means, "Now let's talk about me." I think pastors should employ the same degree of honesty. I told you a story about me. It was funny or sad or whatever, but "now let's talk about God."

Or: *"That story has nothing to do with God, but it was awesome, right?"* Sometimes it's just fun to hear a good story. To laugh and shake off the week with something interesting and hilarious. Maybe that's enough. Maybe it doesn't need some intricately woven connection point that makes the entire crowd say, "He started talking about bunny rabbits made of cotton candy and we didn't know where he was going, but now that he's arrived in Malachi 1:3, I can see what he meant all along. Brilliant." If you've got a good story, just bring it. Drop it off. Say, "This is awesome." Then move on. We're with you. We like awesome too.

COMPLETELY DISREGARDING ALL KNOWN COPYRIGHT LAWS

He's lovin' me

JOHN 3:16

God help us all if we arrive in heaven and there's a patent and trademark office. Seriously, we are screwed. Especially me. Let's be clear, the original idea for the *Stuff _____ Like* format came from Christian Lander, the talented author of the blog and book *Stuff White People Like*. Sometimes I like to pretend that I just sprinkled God flavoring on the idea like the creative think tank that turned Adidas into "Add Jesus." And people will kindly tell me that I created an homage, but usually when I describe the humble origins of the *Stuff Christians Like* blog, I use the less French-sounding phrase, "I ripped off that idea for Jesus."

MID-PRAYER MUSIC THAT MATERIALIZES OUT OF NOWHERE

A closing prayer at church that is not enrobed in some sort of soft musical accompaniment is like one of those hairless cats. Technically speaking, it's still a closing prayer, but it seems naked and you want it to leave the room as quickly as possible.

The most important rule of a prayer duet is that you can't start the song at the very same moment as the prayer. That would seem forced and fake, as if instead of praying, you were putting on *Prayer, the Musical!*

You have to start the music in the middle of the prayer, slowly and quietly, as if the musician playing wasn't intending to play along with the prayer but was so inspired by it that he couldn't help but pick up an instrument in response.

"That is a really beautiful closing prayer our pastor is saying and I've already got this acoustic guitar in my hand. Maybe I'll just play a C chord. Just one, tiny note in response."

But he can't stop there, can he? It's never just one note; it always trickles slowly into a song, and when it does, I'm left with lots of questions in the crowd.

Do they practice that beforehand? Does the minister say to the musician, "When you hear the word 'freedom,' that is your cue"? "Don't miss it. I'm going to trust-fall this prayer back into your hands and I expect a musical blanket to catch it."

Does the drummer ever get mad that he never gets tapped to do the prayer duet? No one ever says, "I need you to come in during the middle of the prayer with the kick drum. Just start beating that thing as loud as you can." And it can't be a harp either. Those things are like musical refrigerators. They're impossible to hide. The minute the congregation sees one on stage they know "prayer song today." There's no surprising people with a harp.

Is it bad that the minute I hear that music starting I try to locate the musician? That's horrible, right? I should be focused on the prayer and God and worship, not trying to "Where's Waldo" the prayer musician. But I can't help it; they keep switching it up on me. Sometimes he's sitting on stage where he's been the whole time, and it's like the words of the prayer awoke him from a deep slumber while the rest of the musicians stay frozen in time. On other Sundays a musician will slowly materialize in the shadows offstage and musically tiptoe their way to the center of the stage like a tag team wrestler coming to relieve his partner. Sometimes you can't ever find them; they're playing somewhere deep within the bowels of the church and their prayer song is floating into the sanctuary like the Phantom of the Opera. Which I usually just assume means they're too ugly for big church. "Sure, go ahead and play for the youth group and children's church, but for this prayer, during the main service, we really feel like this broom closet is going to offer you the best acoustics. So let's just tuck you right in here. Someone will mic your instrument and knock on the door when it's time to start playing."

NOT KNOWING HOW TO HOLD HANDS

"Please join hands" are three of the most terrifying words you'll ever hear a minister say. (Second only to, "We never talk about money at our church, but today ...")

Holding hands isn't difficult. But we tend to violate some simple rules that govern hand-to-hand combat. Let's review the things we should keep in mind when holding hands with strangers at church:

NEVER interlink your fingers.

This is way, way too intimate if you don't know me and your full name isn't "my wife." But some people do it. Instead of the, "Hey pal, I know we're holding hands, which is weird, but oh well," palm-to-palm grip, they weave their fingers between yours. As soon as someone does that, the thirteen-year-old inside me automatically thinks, "This person is trying to make out with me." This isn't a couples-only skate at the roller rink to Bobby Brown's "Tender Roni." Let's never interlink our fingers. Please.

NEVER give the "You're great" squeeze.

For some reason lots of Christians feel the need to punctuate a good handhold with a tiny gesture. They want closure. A fireworks grand finale to the handholding session. I understand that, but please, avoid the temptation to end our time together with a "you're great" squeeze. It's nowhere near as intimate as interlinking, but it still feels creepy coming from a man in his mid-fifties that up until thirty seconds ago I had never seen in

my life. I don't need closure. Our hand relationship is over. I'm
ready to move on. It's not you; it's me.

NEVER linger.

When it becomes clear that the period of handholding is over,
I expect you to ditch my hand like a bank robber fleeing the
scene. Seriously. Let's not be the last people pressed together
with our hands awkwardly connected. Letting go is a race. I
want us to win. Let's set a new land speed record in disconnect-
ing. Come on, we can do it. Eye of the tiger. Eye of the freaking
tiger.

If we ever find ourselves holding hands at an event, I should
warn you that I'll hold you accountable to all of these rules. If
you persist in violating them, I'll probably use my sweat defense
mechanism. I don't know if being sweaty is a spiritual gift, but I
have it. And so will you if you insist on breaking the rules.

SCHEDULING REVIVALS

Revivals, those unexpected outpourings of God that sweep
whole communities up into a heavenly rhythm, are an important part of the Christian faith. Sometimes the best way to
show how important they are is to go ahead and get one on the
calendar.

Sure, they're often spontaneous, but if you can fit one in
right after Vacation Bible School and right before Missions
Month begins, might as well. Every time I see a church that
has "Revival this Sunday 8:00 p.m." on a sign, I imagine God
and Revival playing Connect Four up in heaven and having this
conversation:

> REVIVAL: Oh snap, look at the time. I've gotta bounce.
> I'm supposed to be at Stonehill Church in fifteen
> minutes.

GOD: What? Stonehill? I wasn't going to send you down there until this summer. Are you sure?

REVIVAL: Yeah. Look, it's right there on the sign. You didn't know?

GOD: Of course I knew. I'm God. I was just distracting you from Connect Four. Which you lost. You just got served!

REVIVAL: That seems like a harsh thing for a loving God to say.

GOD: No, you misunderstand. I cleaned up your Connect Four board for you. You got served.

STEALING MEMBERS FROM OTHER CHURCHES

This happens. I know it shouldn't. I know we're supposed to be one big body of believers united in Christ. But sometimes when you want to grow your church, when you want to expand your impact in the community, you might need to apply a sleeper hold to that church down the street.

They're struggling anyway. Their last Vacation Bible School didn't even have a blow-up jump-jump thing. Their parking lot is rarely full, and you heard they don't even use a drummer in their worship music. You're not stealing their members—you're liberating them. This is a mercy acquisition. You're doing it for God.

The best way to steal other members for God is pretty simple. Two words: "Live Animals."

For some reason, we Christians love live animals in church performances. If you can get a real donkey to carry Jesus down the aisle on Palm Sunday or have a live nativity scene with a cow, forget about it. Game over. Other churches in your town don't stand a chance. It raises the holiness and the awesomeness factor exponentially. Think I'm joking? The first two times

I went to the very successful Catalyst Conference, they busted out a camel, a pig, a donkey . . . and an elephant. They understand the rule of live animals.

And if rival churches follow suit, just throw the ultimate animal card: the live Noah's ark performance. I've never heard of anyone doing this, but surely it's not too hard to find someone who owns a couple of birds of prey, a few tigers, and some emus. If you pull off that event, you'll probably need to build a bigger parking lot because you, my friend, are about to be flooded with people from other churches.

COMING TO CHURCH SICK

I can hear you. I can tell that deep down you're trying to hide. Trying to fade into the crowd so no one will notice, but like a horror movie where the phone call is coming from inside the house, I know you're sitting close to me. One row away? Two pews over? It doesn't matter. I know you're there. And I know your dirty little secret . . .

You've got a cold.

You're sniffing. A lot. And it's not even a sad part of the service. If someone was getting baptized I could understand watery eyes, maybe even a runny nose. I'd write off how hard you're hitting those Kleenex to emotion. Baptisms are beautiful. Every time my wife sees one she cries. And then I ask her if we're in a fight and then she tells me, "No, this is a beautiful baptism." I get that, I do.

But you're different today. You've got a wad of Kleenex. You didn't want to bring the whole box because that would be too obvious. That would announce to everyone sitting around you, "Look at me! I refused to take a Sunday off! I'm going to give my offering *and* my cold today!" You couldn't go the box route, and those mini Kleenex packages that are cellophane wrapped and hold approximately 1.7 tissues are useless. So you brought a wad, a shapeless mass of Kleenex that you keep unfolding layers from like a tissue onion. One pocket for clean. One pocket for used. I know the drill.

I'm on to you. At the beginning of service you tried to do all your nose blowing under the cover of loud singing. Like Tim Robbins' character in the movie *Shawshank Redemption* waiting until thunder struck before he tried to break a hole through the pipe that led to freedom, you waited until the chorus of songs to rattle off a loud nose clearing. But then the sermon started and you were stuck. You tried to fight it, to mentally tell your nose, "Be cool, don't drip, be cool." There's a part of us all that thinks this is going to work at first. That if we just concentrate hard enough our nose will stop dripping or a tickle in our throat will stop making us cough if we can just muster enough willpower. It never works though, and you had to wait until the pastor said something funny so you could blow your nose while everyone else was laughing. Hoping perhaps that the crowd's jovial good time would provide an auditory cover for your nose clearing.

It didn't work though, none of it did, because you made one fatal mistake—menthol. Nothing screams "I'm sick" like creating a thick atmosphere of menthol-flavored breath that hovers over a section of seats in church. The problem is that no one recreationally does menthol. Bubblicious does not offer menthol gum. Lollipops don't come in Eucalyptus flavor. If there's menthol in the room, someone is nursing a cold. And the minute I smelled it, I knew it was you.

Now that I've found you. Now that we've locked eyes, I'm going to try to communicate a two-part thought with my head nod. The first part is sympathy: "Hey fella, sorry to see that you're sick; that stinks." That head nod goes up and down. The second head nod, which is side to side, is a little different, "You shouldn't have come to church today. The pastor can't tell you that, but I can. God is okay with you listening to the podcast and not infecting his people, the bride of Christ, with your germs. Seriously, you can stay home next time."

Is that an awful lot to ask of a head nod? Probably, but ultimately it won't matter. You're so hopped up on cold medicine you're probably going to think I'm break dancing. Which is fine, being mistaken as a pop and locker is one of my lifetime aspirations. But know this. I'm watching. I'm listening and above all, I'm trying to hold my breath for forty-five minutes. But it's getting difficult. Just promise me that if I pass out from my David Blaine – like attempt not to breathe your mushroom cloud of menthol, you won't volunteer to do mouth to mouth.

DRINKING COFFEE IN CHURCH

Ten years ago, if you drank coffee during a church service, people knew you as "that coffee guy" or "that tea lady." It wasn't unheard of, but it certainly wasn't as popular as it is today. Now, forgetting your coffee cup before service is like leaving your Bible at home. While the rest of the pew enjoys triple foam Hazelnut Mocha Venti Explosions, you sit there like some sort of drinkless hobo. It's embarrassing.

When I sell out and open up the *Stuff Christians Like* gift shop, I'm going to sell a Bible with a hollowed-out spine that you can put coffee in. There will be a little screw-top spout and when you need a sip, you can just tip your Bible back. You'll look really holy because people will think you're literally kissing your Bible during church.

WISHING YOU HAD AN EASY JOB, LIKE WORKING AT A CHURCH

Don't you wish you worked at a church? That would be such a dream job!

I've never been blessed that way but my assumption is that other than Sunday, a church job is kind of like having a really long quiet time. You probably get to read the Bible all day and take long breaks in your prayer closet and spend eight hours a day growing your own spiritual life.

I'm sure the phone rings sometimes, like when someone needs a casserole of hope after a death in the family or a youth group van breaks down, but for the most part I imagine the average day is filled with a lot of "me time."

And God is your boss. How cool is that? There's no politics or in-fighting or gossip like at the average corporate job. It's just a collection of people, a family really, living out of the gifts God has given them. Loving on each other. (You actually work at a place where "love on" is an acceptable verb!) Everyone is all on the same page, pouring out to each other the love that God is pouring into them. Don't you want to hug this book right now just thinking about that?

I bet there's always an acoustic guitar being played somewhere in the office. (Should we even call where people work at a church an "office"? Let's call it a "happy holy spot" instead.) And when you go to make copies on the printer, you'll hear the acoustic guitar and probably join an impromptu sing-along right there in the mailroom and make up a song.

Is it even really a full-time job? Seriously, other than maybe a few hours on a Sunday morning, what else are you doing? Praying? Worshipping? Holding car washes to raise money for mission trips? What's that take, four hours, tops? How do you spend the rest of the week?

Being loved on I bet. See, there it is again! That's the kind of thing that is constantly happening if you work at a church, but good luck trying to say that at a real job. If tomorrow in one of my meetings at work I said, "I really need to love on these third-quarter budget estimates," I would immediately get "laughed on" by my co-workers. Not if you work at a church. They support each other!

Plus, they've got an entire congregation full of people that love them unconditionally. Imagine having hundreds of people that are fans of what you do and how you do it. People that are going to wholeheartedly accept what you do and never write mean emails no matter if they disagree with your decisions. Me? I read negative opinions from our customers all the time. People that work at churches? They're opening thank-you notes and sunshine emails and gift baskets with delicious cheeses and spiced meats all day long.

Someday, if they ever sunset my job (a fun-sounding euphemism we're actually now using to replace the word "eliminate"), maybe I'll get a church job and get to live the sweet life.

PRESSING ON YOUR EYES DURING PRAYER

Does this practice have an age limit? When you hit your thirties, is it biblically illegal to press your fingers against your eyes so hard when you pray that you see a light show? Is that something you're supposed to leave in childhood?

I hope not, because this experience is delightful. I remember sitting through long prayers as a child, my hands on my face, bored. To overcome my boredom, I'd press against my tightly clutched eyelids until sparks and colors would flutter by.

I secretly believed that if I pressed hard enough, maybe I would see Jesus. That the shapes and hues would slowly form his face. It never happened. Which is probably a good thing, because if I had seen the face of Jesus, other people probably would have wanted to come see it too. I'd have a line of Jesus fans, trying to get near my eyes, lighting candles near me, and eventually I'd have to auction my eyelids on eBay. Which would be awkward and probably a little painful because from that moment on I'd be some weird-looking guy without any eyelids. I'd look wide awake and excited 24/7.

Not pressing   Pressing just the   Pressing
hard enough   right amount   too hard

WORSHIP EAGLES

Other than some unexpected sex advice from an older gentleman and my father, the minister, initially forgetting to give us our rings, my wedding was fairly normal. My friend's wedding, however, her wedding was extraordinary.

She married a great guy that is a Bible scholar. One of the ways he honored this deep love for God's Word is by having an eagle in his wedding.

Go ahead and read that last sentence again. It's a big one.

While most people plan candle moments and have their silver medal friend that was not good enough to be in the wedding party read "love is patient," this guy actually hired an eagle to make a cameo. Now, there's some debate about whether it was an eagle or a hawk. I think that's kind of like arguing about whether it was a shark or a barracuda that bit your foot off while swimming. The details don't matter nearly as much as the fact that he had a bird of prey in his wedding.

My brother went and said that he spent most of the wedding filming action scenes in his head in which the eagle swooped down and flew off with the flower girl. It didn't though. Apparently it sat up next to the minister on a tall perch looking all "eagly" and just chilling, with a look on its face that kind of said, "Yeah, I'm an eagle. Don't sweat the technique."

The reason my friend loves eagles is due in large part to the Bible verse in Isaiah 40:31 that says, "They shall mount up with wings as eagles" (KJV). And he's not alone. I found forty-one eagle-themed products on a Christian website once.

But I don't think that's enough. I don't think we've worked enough eagle into our lives. So I prepared a short list of ways I think having an eagle on staff could help a church.

Interpretive Dance

Can you imagine how amazing it would be to have a live eagle fly around your sanctuary while people did an interpretive dance routine to Bette Midler's song "Wind beneath My Wings"? I'm starting to tear up a little right now just thinking about seeing him unfurl his wings as sweet Bette sings "Flyyyyy, flyyyyyyy, fly high against the sky ...."

The Seat Saver

I personally am not a huge fan of that guy or girl that saves nineteen seats at church with a variety of papers and Bibles and purses. We do all this work to get visitors to come to church and then tell them they can't sit here, here, or right there. An eagle would fix that. I would have our falcon master (you would need to add that position to your church regardless of whether an eagle is considered a falcon; someone needs to wear that big leather glove) teach the eagle how to pick up the junk people use to save seats. Just as you put down a trail of bulletins across some seats you wanted to save, a missile of feathers and talons and beak would swoop down from the heavens and steal every one of them.

The Crying Kid

Occasionally, someone feels their kid is too old or young or tired or delicate to attend childcare or Sunday school. So they bring him in the church, squirt Capri Suns down his throat for energy, and then pretend they don't hear him wailing through the entire service. Oh, but the eagle hears. The eagle hears all. With the softest approach in the game, the eagle would lightly pick up the child, carry him away, and drop him in a ball pit outside with all the other crying kids. (Am I the only one who thinks this way?)

The Hype Man

Instead of having that guy/girl on staff that is in charge of randomly yelling "amen" during the sermon to get the crowd going, you could use the eagle. Whenever you made a good point or wanted to increase the energy in the room, you could have the eagle do that loud, piercing scream they are known for. No one would ever doze off in church again. Although some pastors would abuse it and overuse the worship eagle like the way I once abused the phrase "if by." I was constantly saying stuff like, "Am I hungry? No, *if by* 'no' you mean hungry enough to eat my shoes." My younger brothers, Will and Bennett, had to have a joke intervention. It was a very unfunny season in my life.

AWAY-GAME BAPTISMS

When I was a kid, our church spent Labor Day weekend at Camp Resolute, a small boy scout facility on the edge of town with tents, a mess hall, and all the things that make camps fun. Besides having great campfires, which make for fantastic testi-whoanies (that awkward over-sharing people feel compelled to do in the presence of open flame), it had a lake. I liked swimming and canoeing, but my favorite lake activity was the away-game baptisms for a few very distinct reasons:

Wildlife is in the mix.

The chances of a turtle popping up in your baptismal at church are pretty slim. During an away game, that's completely possible. It's not the turtles you should be afraid of though ... it's the snakes. Imagine a huge water moccasin slipping across that glassy surface, just as you're about to usher someone under water. Do you call off the baptism and write the church folklore right then, or would you allow the urban legend about the "guy's baptism that was almost ruined by a serpent from the devil" to grow naturally over time?

It's unscripted.

Our church records some amazing videos of people before they're baptized. Usually, they get four or five takes to get the message right because everyone gets nervous in front of the camera. The final take is always really touching, but part of me misses the days when you could just blurt out whatever was in your heart (or mouth). It was awesome to see my dad, a minister, try to rein it back in when someone dropped a wild sentence about how crazy life was before Jesus came into their picture.

The "THAT guy's getting baptized?" guy shows up.

Rarely does someone crash the baptismal at church. Those things are planned and orchestrated. Our baptismal is twenty feet in the air above the crowd. A person would have to scale the wall like Spider-Man if they wanted to pool hop. The church can prepare for whoever's getting baptized each Sunday. But in away-game baptisms, anything goes. Each year, at least one guy who came to the camp just because he likes camping would be sitting on the dock while my dad baptized other people. And he'd realize, "I'm here. I have a bathing suit on. Why not?" Next thing you know, he was wading over to my dad, and a murmur of "*that* guy's getting baptized?" would ripple through the crowd.

If I ever start a church, I'm doing 100% away-game baptisms. I'll probably try to do them in some sort of body of water that qualifies as a "holler." I'm not sure if that's a cross between a pond and a swimming hole, but something about having a T-shirt that says, "I got holy at the holler" sounds pretty nice. Or maybe we'll baptize people in the crick so we can say, "I got Christ in the crick." Is it wrong to arrange destination baptisms in the same way people get married in tropical resorts just so I can make horribly puntastic T-shirts?

Do you ever think God lets Moses win at Frisbee golf? The guy didn't even get to enter the Promised Land after forty years of wandering; would it be so much to let him win at least once? Or would the purity of God's character prevent him from deliberately missing a shot? That's the kind of tough call that most theologians refuse to make. Not me. Moses always loses to God but he crushes Samson, who by the way is all drive, no short game.

FEARING THAT GOD WILL SEND YOU TO AFRICA IF YOU GIVE HIM YOUR ENTIRE LIFE

It's a well-known Christian fact that if you surrender your life to God—if you *really* turn over your hopes and dreams to him and *truly* give him control of your entire life—the first thing he's going to do is send you to Africa. Immediately.

You'll go from 0 to Hut in about 3.9 seconds. So if you don't like the idea of being insanely poor and living in the desert in a thatch lean-to and eating—I don't know—a steady diet of bugs, you should probably not give God everything you've got.

Because it's a safe bet that if becoming a missionary in Africa is the most miserable thing you can imagine happening to you, that's probably the first thing God is going to do when you become a Christian.

Of course if you *really* believe that if you turned your life over to God he would immediately send you somewhere you'd hate, then that's a pretty hateful God you've got on your hands. If the very first thing God is going to do when you ask him to take the wheel is crash your car into a tree or a deep ravine, you're serving a pretty miserable God.

That subtle reference to the Carrie Underwood song "Jesus Take the Wheel" would have killed three years ago and made you think I'm really relevant, but when I gave my life to God he said I had to use old references to country songs, which is the writer's equivalent to being sent to a literary hut. But that's just how God is.

SEEING GOD IN NATURE

Seeing God in nature is one of our favorite things to do. We love holding retreats in places like the mountains or the beach. Something about a panoramic view really drives home the point that "God is big. If he can handle how the ocean works, he can take care of my little problem." But a panoramic view is only half the battle. What we really like is when we can find a cross shape that has naturally formed somewhere on God's green earth. Two trees that have grown together, a formation of rocks that kind of looks like a wobbly cross, that clump of stars out in the dead of space that resembles a cross. We love finding reminders of God in nature.

I think that's great, except that the last time I went to the beach, on the roof deck of the house my family rented, I tried to force God to meet my schedule. I got up early, took my note-book and pen up there, held my breath as the sun came up, and ... nothing. So I literally walked the entire deck to make sure I was not in the wrong God spot, as if maybe the God juice was flowing to the corner I wasn't standing in.

And when it didn't happen, I tried to help God out by priming the pump. "Wow, that water is endless. Maybe you want to tell me about your endless love? No, nothing there? How about all the shells that are scattered across the sand when the tide goes out? Maybe you want to talk about how the search for wisdom is a lot like searching for a perfect shell amongst a million broken ones? How's that sound? Nothing, hmmm. Let's think about the dunes or storms or something. Help me out, God; I'm doing all the work here."

I was at the beach so I expected a God performance, for him to speak something deep and beautiful into my heart. But he didn't. I didn't leave the beach that day with any new insights, even though I probably could have written a pretty amazing sequel to "Footprints in the Sand" called "Footprints 2: The Revenge."

TELLING TESTIMONIES THAT ARE EXCITING RIGHT UP UNTIL THE MOMENT YOU BECAME A CHRISTIAN

"You should have seen me before I became a Christian. I was wild. I had this really hot girlfriend who was named after a city, and we were living in this cool loft downtown and every night, not just on the weekends, *every* night, we were going out. Her uncle owned a bunch of nightclubs and a fleet of yachts, so we would just party and then get on one of the yachts and have the craziest times and catch fresh crabs in the Florida Keys and then watch the sun pierce the morning sky with streaks of red and orange and yellow.

"And then I became a Christian. The end."

No one ever says "the end" when they tell a reverse testimony, one of those rare gems that buckets all the exciting parts of a life story before the moment of salvation, but they should. Because that's what they're doing. They're essentially saying, "I used to have a really fun life and then I became a Christian. The end."

We associate all the fun and excitement and neon coolness of life with the world and leave God all the boring, discipline-flavored moments. He's like eating broccoli. We know it's good for us, but it's still broccoli. But that can't be right. God is wild. He's constantly saying, "Let's go find cliffs to jump off of," and, "I know exactly what you need, because, guess what, I put that need there." He created my heart and the deepest desires I have, and there's no yacht or nightclub on the planet that can access those spots of me like God can.

And besides, he invented sex. And not just "let's make a baby" sex—he invented "whoa, the world just tilted on its axis; I can't believe we get to do that and go to heaven too" sex. Sometimes we act like we were the ones that discovered it was fun, like maybe God was in heaven and was surprised to see how enjoyable we were able to make it. "Whoa, I created that for procreation purposes; I had no idea it would be so awesome." And so we give the world credit for sex and think that God is only down with the functional version, but the fun version, the wild version, that's probably something Marvin Gaye came up with.

PRETENDING THAT IF GOD SPOKE TO YOU AUDIBLY, EVERYTHING IN YOUR LIFE WOULD INSTANTLY FALL INTO PLACE

If I were God, which my counselor Chuck assures me is not the case, I would probably want to pile drive everyone who ever complained that "God has never spoken to me."

And that would be quite the pile driver-a-thon, just a non-stop beat down with T-shirts and pony rides for the family members who weren't receiving a pile driver. Because not hearing from God is one of our favorite things to complain about.

I think Christians do this because we all know at least one person who says, "I heard God speak to me, clear as day, and it changed my life forever." And if they're humble, they only say it when prompted, but if they're not, they drop that sentence if they get within ten miles of a conversation having anything remotely to do with God. (Which could indicate that their life didn't really change, but that's beside the point.)

It's possible God dropped some solid, audible wisdom into that person's life. Maybe he megaphoned them like Paul on the road to Damascus. But when we hear stories like that, we twist them all around in our heads. We don't hear, "I heard God speak to me, clear as day, and it changed my life." We hear, "Unless God speaks to you too, your life will never be changed." So we establish that as the gold standard of radical life change and secretly walk around having internal conversations like this:

"Is that you, God? Are you there? I thought for a second I heard you. Okay, let me know if you want to talk. I'm ready. Say something out loud, please. Speak up. Just this once. Come on."

We'll complain to our friends, "God's never spoken to me. Yeah, in the Bible, I guess, but he's never really spoken to me directly." That might be true. He might never speak to you audibly, but getting hung up on that is such a fantastic way to short-change the Bible. "Yeah, it's good ... it's hundreds of pages of

#227   **Narnia.**

God's Word, but not like that one magical, silver-bullet, audible sentence I'm waiting for. That ... that would change everything."

BEING SLIGHTLY ANNOYED WHEN GOD ASKS FOR MORE THAN 10 PERCENT OF YOUR MONEY

Huh? What was that last thing you said, God? You want me to give what to who? Uh yeah, this is awkward. I didn't want to do this, but can you come over here and look at Quicken with me? It's financial software that shows where my money is going, and it was invented by ... I'm explaining things to God. Ha, ha, this is so silly, but still.

See right here, this column that says "tithe"? It's automatic. I am automatically firing off a direct deposit to church every month for 10 percent of my salary. Pretty nice, right? But I could swear I just heard you ask me to give more than 10 percent.

Which is weird because you and I are kind of locked into a lifetime 90/10 contract. I keep 90. You keep 10. I'd like to change that, I would; that sounds great, in theory. But 10 percent is in the Bible. And I'm not ready to go against the Bible, soooo let's just stick with our current agreement.

ENCOURAGING THE DOWNTRODDEN BY REMINDING THEM, "GOD DOESN'T PROMISE US AN EASY LIFE"

The best way to make someone having a really horrible day feel even worse is to say, "God didn't promise you an easy life." It's such a great beat-down sentence because in the very same stroke you punch both God and your friend in the face. On the one hand, you shame your friend for complaining: "Hey, you diva Christian, it's not going to be all bon bons and bling-ity bling easy living with God. I feel like you should have known this simple truth of faith by now." And then you also throw God under the bus: "I know you're miserable and you think your life is horrible, but that's just how God rolls. He's a big fan of your personal misery, so get used to it. That's how he gets down."

NAME-DROPPING GOD TO GET OUT OF A SPEEDING TICKET

I've never gotten a speeding ticket, but if I ever do, I want to be honest with you. I'm going to name-drop God. Not just a little bit. I'm going to name-drop God so hard and so often in that conversation with the cop that God in heaven is going to stop playing Battleship with Peter and say, "Hold up, did someone just give me a shout-out? Is it the Grammys already?"

You probably don't think that's biblical, but then you probably also forget Philippians 4:13, which says, "I can do all things through Christ who strengthens me" (NKJV). And since that verse clearly gives me the freedom to get out of a speeding ticket, I'm going to name-drop Christ, too. I'll go through the whole Trinity if that's what it takes to get out of the ticket.

You can, too, if you'd like. It's pretty easy. Here's what to say, depending on the circumstances, if you get pulled over:

After church on Sunday afternoon ...

"Why, hello officer. I was just coming from church, where we had some baptisms and prayed. There were baby dedications too. Did I mention that? Sweet little babies. Was I speeding?"

On Sunday night ...

"Hello, officer! My, where has the day gone? You start out with a church service, and helping people and singing songs to Jesus, and end up just getting so busy on the Sabbath that you end up speeding around. Was I going too fast? And is today technically the Sabbath? I always get confused about that."

On Thursday night at three in the morning ...
"Hello, officer. Beautiful night, isn't it? You certainly can see God's handiwork on nights like this, what with all the twinkling stars and the quiet whispers of the happy crickets in the tall grass. Reminds me of a retreat I went on one weekend after helping feed the homeless. Holy Spirit, communion, Jesus. Were you saying something about a ticket?"

Technically even if it's Thursday and you go to church on Sunday, you're "on your way to church." It's just going to take you three days to get there. If that police officer decides to interpret "on my way to church" to mean "I'm headed to church *right now,* so please don't impede my immediate progress to God's house ..." well, that's really just between you and the officer. Just don't give me a shout-out if you end up in jail for providing false information to the police. Save your one phone call for someone who's smart and won't tell you to name-drop the Alpha and Omega to get out of a speeding ticket. That's horrible advice. You don't want that guy handling your case.

Of course I should warn you that I wrote this book while living in the Bible Belt of America. My friend got pulled over doing 150 mph in a Porsche on his way to volunteer with high school students one Sunday morning in Atlanta. The cop screamed at him for a while, took a look at his volunteer T-shirt, and waved him on.

REFUSING TO TITHE UNTIL YOU HAVE THE PROPER AMOUNT OF CHEERFULNESS IN YOUR HEART

Given the chance, I would probably edit every word I have ever written in my life. For some reason, seeing something I wrote makes me want to either throw up or punch the piece of paper

132 STUFF CHRISTIANS LIKE

directly in the face. I think I could have done something differently or better. I want to start over, I want to rewrite, I want to
edit.

I don't think God has that problem when he looks at the Bible.
I don't think he has any problems, but if he did want to edit one
verse, like just a tiny edit—I'm talking a single word—I think
I know which one he would yank. "Cheerful." He would delete
the word "cheerful" from 2 Corinthians 9:7 about him wanting a
cheerful giver because man, oh man, have we abused that one.

Have you ever met someone who didn't want to give money
to the church or a charity until they had a cheerful heart? They
waited until they were cheerful enough to throw their tithe in? I
have, and that person's name is "me."

I know that's dumb, but I used to lie to myself, saying things
like, "I don't want to fake my tithe. It says it right there in the
Bible, God wants a cheerful giver. What, are you telling me to go
against God's Holy Word? No, it's not evident in my life that I'm
following many of God's other holy precepts, but this ... this is
one I'm passionate about."

That's ridiculous logic, but the thing that's even crazier is
the idea that we can measure cheerfulness. If you're waiting
until you're cheerful enough, what sorts of measurements are
you taking? I'm assuming you're recording the data in either
rainbows or sunshines, but how many sunshines are we talking
about until you can give money to God?

What's your criteria? Mine is the degree to which a person
is smiling. That's how I quantify cheerfulness. Here's what it
looks like:

Full frown

If you've got a huge frown on your face like an open umbrella,
and emo music is considered cotton-candy-happy compared to
you, then you probably shouldn't give that Sunday. You're not
ready. Use your money instead to buy an apology card for the
owner of the puppy you kicked on the way to church.

Flat face

You are a stoic fortress of solitude. No one can discern your feelings. Are you deeply happy? Are you in the throes of some great personal tragedy? No one can tell because your face is so flat and expressionless. But maybe, just maybe, there's some small degree of cheerfulness brewing beneath that cold exterior. Feel free to throw some coins in the offering basket. Not quarters. You're not ready for quarters. Let's not get crazy, but put in as many dimes as you can fit in your pocket without looking like you have a sock full of coins you're going to hit someone with like Charles Bronson. Your face is so hard to read, I don't want to put anything past you.

Sly smirk

That's a smile, sort of. You're doing that sarcastic grin that people like me do in photos. You're too cool to flat-out smile, but you don't want to look like some super serious guy who takes himself all serious all the serious time, so you went middle of the road. It's almost as if you're laughing at an ironic joke you heard about an ironic T-shirt from a guy wearing an ironic winter hat in the middle of July. That's borderline happy, my friend. Feel free to throw some actual paper money in. You've reached dollar-bill cheerfulness.

Massive smile

I didn't think it was going to happen this quickly, but based on the huge I-don't-care-what-anyone-else-thinks, life-is-wonderful smile you've got going on, I would say you're officially ready to give. And I don't just mean coins or a few dollars. I'm talking about real giving, in envelopes. Honest-to-goodness envelopes that have your name printed on them so that everyone around you can see how cheerful you are. Because they don't just give envelopes to anyone. There's an application process and a cheerfulness test that's very similar to this one, although it involves breathing into a tube, but it's a licorice tube so it ends up being pretty nice.

PUTTING GOD ON YOUR BUSINESS CARD

What does it mean when your house painter has a Jesus fish on his business card? Should I think that means he's going to be really trustworthy? Or maybe detailed and passionate about his work? Is there some scene in the Bible where Jesus does a really good job painting someone's two-story great room? Because that's what I'm looking for right now—just a normal painter who has workers who don't have prison tats officially indicating that they've killed someone. Is that what the cross on the side of his painting van means? Very little chance of getting murdered during the course of the project? So many questions, so few answers.

Some of my favorite businesses are Christian, but they tell you that through their actions, not their business cards. The worst time I ever got ripped off was by a super loud, formerly church-employed Christian. Whenever someone tries to validate someone's quality simply by saying, "He'll do a great job. He's a Christian," my first thought is, "I am so screwed."

TELLING GOD, "THANKS IN ADVANCE FOR YOUR COOPERATION."

I love when people thank me for doing something I haven't done yet. They'll send me an email, ask me to work on a project, and then end the message by saying, "Thanks in advance for your cooperation."

Ohh, that is tricky. That bold move is designed to force my hand, to make me sit there and think, "Well they already thanked me for doing it. I suppose I should in fact do it."

Even better though is when there is a condition of speed applied to the request. "Thank you for doing this so quickly," or, "I really appreciate your quick turnaround." That's two levels of trickery. Not only have I not agreed to do it, but I certainly haven't agreed to do it quickly. If you want to add a third level, get God into the mix and tell someone, "Thank you for serving the kingdom of God with your talents." That's church talk for, "We're not going to pay you any money for that thing we need you to do, but we are going to thank you in a way that makes it next to impossible to say no. What, you don't want to serve the kingdom of God?"

That's pretty ridiculous, but sometimes I do the same thing. Instead of asking God for his guidance or praying about where/what/how he would have me move through a situation, I throw him a little advance appreciation.

"God, thank you for blessing this book. Thank you for allowing me to sell more copies than *The Shack*. Thank you for allowing me to become the first Christian author to ever host *Saturday Night Live*. Thank you for all of that."

WITNESSING

I've never found what I thought was a ten dollar bill on the ground but was actually a tract disguised as a ten dollar bill and thought to myself, "Phew, I thought that was going to be free money. Let's see what this tricky but potentially life changing piece of paper has to say today."

THE BAIT AND SWITCH

Hi, how are you? Do you mind if I ask you a question?

Do you like pizza, soda, and allowing the blood of Jesus to purify you of all your sins?

What? What did I say? You don't like pizza?

That's what the sweaty minister from the singing group my pastor father brought to town one year should have said in the middle of their bait and switch event.

Sure, the ACLU would have still been called. Sure, the local newspaper would have still crucified my old man. Sure, the hundreds of kids that heard the singing group perform Beach

Boy songs during assemblies at public schools would have still been surprised when the doors at the Friday night event were closed with guards that discouraged them from leaving until the altar call was over.

All of those things might have still happened even if the minister had been up front with us, but at least we would have known that "Pizza Blast" might not be the best name for the event. Looking back at what shotgunned from that stage once the Kokomo gloves were off, I have to think that "Jesus Blast" might have been a more appropriate name.

FEELING GUILTY FOR NOT CONVERTING ENOUGH PEOPLE

I don't know what "enough" is, but I know I haven't reached it. I don't have any numbers to support this theory; rarely do my friends and I sit around and count the people we've led to Christ. But in my head, I imagine every other Christian on the planet being wildly more successful at converting people than I am. They've led both sales teams at work to the Lord, witnessed to three of the four cul-de-sacs in their neighborhood, and left a trail of believers at every fast food drive-thru they've ever ordered at. And me, I could count the people I've converted on one hand.

I have a plan though. I have a "Hail Mary" pass I'll throw that will balance everything out. It's kind of a secret though, so lean in close for this next part . . . I'm going to convert a celebrity.

I know, I know, it's brilliant, right?

Celebrities count more right now in society than normal people, and that's kind of true in Christian circles too. How many times have you had a conversation with friends and someone will say, "Can you imagine what it would be like if Kid Rock became a Christian? Wow, imagine what that would do for God's kingdom if that happened." Sure God's probably thinking, "Kid Rock? Oh you mean, Robert James Ritchie? I love him. Bring him along and his next-door neighbor Mike Smith too. Both of those guys are really important to me." But regardless of the heaven technicalities, I'm still going to focus exclusively on converting the already famous.

I'll just lay low until I finally have access to Kid Rock, and then when I get to heaven God will say, "I know the great commission says everyone; it says 'all nations,' but Kid Rock is pretty dope. So we'll call it even. Get in here, you."

THE SEARCH FOR "ONE MORE PERSON"

One of our favorite things to do during an altar call is to wait for "One More Person." Here's what a minister usually says at about minute seven of the altar call:

"Thank you for heeding the Lord's call this morning. We're going to play one more chorus of 'I Could Sing of Your Love Forever,' and then we're going to end the service. But there's one more person that needs to come down today. One more person waiting for the right moment. Today is it, friend. Right now is your chance. Come home. We'll wait for you."

Every time I experience this phenomenon, I think the same three things:

1. What if the "One More Person" is actually the same jerk in every church? What if it's some dude who hates God so much that he goes around to a bunch of churches just to set off the minister's "spidey sense" and then refuses to come down?
2. Is it wrong to be a little antsy? Have you ever been hungry for lunch and looked around the crowd when you're supposed to have your eyes closed and thought, "Come on, 'One More Person,' let's do this thing. It's noon already!"

3. Would I probably have a fast pass to hell if not for the grace of God because I'm prioritizing lunch over someone's salvation?

WAITING UNTIL A CO-WORKER IS AWAY FROM HIS DESK TO DROP OFF SOME CHRISTIAN PROPAGANDA

In my defense, and perhaps yours too, I didn't set my alarm early to get to work before my colleague did so that I could leave that sermon CD series on his desk. Sure I see him every day and we have email conversations, IM chats, phone calls, and meetings. Sure, I could have placed the sermon series directly in his hand during any of the dozens of interactions we have each week. So then why the cloak and dagger move when I decided he might like to hear a sermon I got from my church?

I was afraid if I did it in person he would pull an "instant return to sender."

I'd hand it to him, he'd take one look at it, realize someone is asking him to recreationally, voluntarily listen to a sermon outside of church, just for fun, and then he'd say, "Yeah, no thanks. Here you go."

Then I'd be left standing there with the CD in my hand, feeling like God just got shot blocked, and trying to find a good segue out of that awkward moment. "Sooo, Atlanta traffic? What's that all about? Crazy, right, what with the whole Beep! Beep! and the Vroooommmm! Anyway, I gotta go."

So instead I opted for the secret drop off when I knew he wouldn't be at work yet. Another great move is to IM a co-worker, ask if he's at his desk, confirm that he's not, write the "Sorry I missed you at your desk" Post-It note ahead of time in your cubicle so that you don't waste time at the scene of the drop, and then sprint back to your desk. That move works too.

Of course now it's been a few months since I did the drop off and neither one of us has mentioned the CD. Every time I visit his cubicle for a work-related issue, I see it sitting in the corner of his desk, Post-It note still attached, mocking me.

It's about being bold for the Lord really.

WHEN PEOPLE YOU'VE KNOWN FOR YEARS ACT SURPRISED WHEN THEY LEARN THAT YOU LOVE JESUS

A surefire way to tell that you're bombing miserably as a Christian is when a friend or co-worker responds to something godly you said with this line:

"Oh, I didn't know that faith was such a big part of your life."

If you don't feel like a completely sweaty heathen at that point, then you missed what they're saying. Let me translate for you. Your friend just said:

"Wow, that godly thing you said comes as a complete surprise to me. Everything about your life screams, 'I don't care about God or faith or church or donating money and blankets to orphans.' I assumed, based on our extensive history together as friends, that you were as undecided on the whole God thing as I am. I would have never guessed you were big-time into faith or Jesus or whatever it is you're into. Completely blew me away. So ... how long have you had this hobby?"

USING THE DESIRE TO BE "CULTURALLY RELEVANT" AS AN EXCUSE TO WATCH *FAMILY GUY*

Do I love the *Family Guy* television cartoon or the new Lil Wayne album? No. But what can I do? Christianity needs to be more relevant. How are we going to change today's generation if we don't understand them? How can I witness to someone about the love of Christ if I can't hang in a conversation about *Family Guy*?

Seriously, what if I'm in the middle of walking someone through the gospel and they say, "That redeeming blood of Jesus thing you're talking about is interesting, but let me ask you something. Who's your favorite character on *Family Guy*?" and I can't instantly answer, "Glen Quagmire"? The whole conversation would break down right there. I'd look out of touch, probably seem a little like a Bible-thumpin' fundamentalist, and God would lose his chance to reach one more person. Is that what you want? You want heaven all to yourself? You're so selfish.

Don't judge my choices. I'm doing this for us. For all of Christianity. I'm going to make us more relevant one episode of *Family Guy* at a time until hopefully, bit by bit, people will start to see that we're not the "I" word. You know which "I" word I mean—the one that for modern Christians is like garlic for a vampire: "Irrelevant." Even saying it out loud makes me feel a little dirty.

GIVING OUT TRACTS INSTEAD OF HALLOWEEN CANDY

I wasn't given a single tract or "Here's-why-you-should-love-Jesus" booklet in my neighborhood last year during Halloween. Living in Georgia, the Bible Belt, I expected at least one. I thought that surely when my daughters dumped out their massive bags of candy on the floor, we'd see one floating in the sea of sweets. We didn't, and I accept the blame. Clearly I've done a poor job converting my neighborhood.

I didn't give one out, either. But I did receive a Halloween tract once in Blowing Rock, North Carolina, and I have to tell you, it was perfectly executed. How can I say that? Because whoever gave it to me followed the simple rules of Halloween Tract Distribution:

Be on theme.

There are a million types of tracts to choose from. If you're going to give one out at Halloween, make sure it's appropriately themed. The one we got on Halloween was about little kids dressing up as ghosts. Had it been about Easter or just a general "Think-Hell-will-be-hot-enough-for-you?" tract, I would have thrown it away instantly. So make sure you stay on theme.

Bag it.

A tract should never travel alone. It should always ride shotgun in a bag with a piece of candy. Otherwise, it's going to be mistaken for a Wendy's fast food coupon for a free drink if you purchase a hamburger or some other such nonsense.

Buy good candy.

You think God wants to travel around in a bag with "M&N's," off-brand M&M's, or those generic black and orange taffies Walmart sells by the gross during Halloween? Doubtful. Make sure you throw your tract in with a Twix or Skittles. Or even better, both. You're always thinking about how to add excellence to your worship service — well, apply that same logic here. That tract had better be surrounded by fantastical candy.

These tips are critical, and I applaud that stranger in Blowing Rock for executing them so flawlessly. Not only did we eat delicious candy when we opened the tract bag, but the tract was well themed. I read the whole thing, and my daughter even colored it with crayons. That's a home run in tract land if ever there was one. (Granted, a deep, lasting relationship with Jesus

144 STUFF CHRISTIANS LIKE

is really a tract grand slam, but I'm already down with the King, so the best they were getting from me was a home run.)

But there's one tip more important than all of those that you need to remember when it comes to proper Halloween tract distribution:

> The moment you give one out, you become the Christian in your neighborhood.

If you weren't known for that before, you are now. If you enjoyed a life of anonymity prior to that, where you could be a jerk and people would just think, "Wow, that guy's a jerk!" those days are over.

Now, when you put three different handwritten complaints in the mailbox of the widow across the street because her dog uses the bathroom in your yard, she'll think, "Wow, that guy *and* God are jerks." That changes things significantly. Which is why I can't hand out a tract until I go apologize to that lady. Hypothetically speaking, of course.

SAYING "YOU'RE IN MY THOUGHTS AND PRAYERS"

Chances are, at some point in a Christian's working career, some tragedy is going to befall a co-worker. And when a Christian gets an interoffice email about it from the administrative assistant, they're tempted to reply with, "I'll pray for them."

Yikes, slow down, Billy Graham!

That kind of behavior might have been acceptable in the sixties—the *1860s*—but these days, you can't just go throwing around the "P" word. Yes, you should be quietly, *secretly* praying for the people you work with, but here are two rules you have to follow unless you want to be chased out of the office as the resident Puritan:

Always say "thoughts and prayers."

For some reason, the phrase "thoughts and" makes it totally acceptable for you to talk about prayer. In a Hallmark or Lifetime Channel kind of way, that phrase mellows out the undertones of "Jesus" many people detect in the word "prayers." Or maybe it's because we like things in pairs. Hugs and kisses. Peanut butter and jelly. Thoughts and prayers. I'm not sure what it is, but you should try it sometime. If you have to tell a co-worker you're going to pray for them, make sure you say, "You'll be in my thoughts *and* prayers."

Never say "Jesus."

I think that the trillions of sneezes that have been followed by the phrase "God bless you" have cleared the way for us to drop this phrase as much as we want in emails. Go hog wild with this God bless you. Use it in the subject line. Put it in the first sentence of the email. Wrap the whole thing up by just repeating, "God bless you. God bless you. God bless you." You'll be fine with that. But if the "J" word slips in for a cameo—even tucked down in the bottom of the P.S.—you're in trouble.

I hope you'll follow these simple rules and not ruin things for the rest of us who have spent the last several years completely neutralizing any form of faith in our interoffice email communications. And if you choose not to, you'll be in my thoughts and prayers ... to Jesus.

BEING THE TOKEN CHRISTIAN

When a co-worker's condo flooded, I was blamed. Not directly, you understand. I didn't break her pipes or make them back up from the street and ruin her hardwood floors. But in our team meeting, when we ran through the list of calamities that had occurred to us over the last six months, one guy I work with said, "What's going on? I thought you had us covered."

Fair question. I'm the token Christian at work, someone people like to keep around to prevent just such inconveniences. Had I been doing a better job, one I inherited because I keep a Bible on my desk, perhaps I could have saved my co-worker from having to retile her kitchen.

But the magical umbrella of protection from things like floods—and the less common but equally dangerous rain of locusts—is not really the token Christian's primary role. Your chief duty is to pray at weddings.

As the token Christian at a wedding, you'll probably just be praying at the reception, and you're going to want to keep it high-level. Think "God lite." They asked you to pray, kind of like they asked their friend that knows how to play the piano if he would play a song during the ceremony. It wasn't an invitation for him to perform a forty-seven-minute-long concerto piece that draws tears and changes the entire crowd's perception of classical music. *Bravissimo!* You have to resist that urge to convert everyone at the wedding in one fell swoop with your token Christian prayer.

Be honest. Be brief. And avoid the phrase "sin nailed to the cross" at all costs. That's only going to freak out the people waiting for you to finish so they can eat cake and do the electric slide.

TERRIFYING PEOPLE INTO A RELATIONSHIP WITH JESUS

A friend of mine attended a children's service once where they did the *Fear Factor* approach to salvation. They sat a roomful of kids, ages six and up, in front of a huge backlit white sheet. In a silhouette on stage, you could see a person lying on an operating table. Suddenly, another silhouette fired up a real chain saw and started cutting the person in half. The person getting chain sawed wailed and flailed in agony as a children's minister told the kids, "This is what God does when he removes sin from your life." From the guts of the person, things like a television, a radio, and other sinful items were pulled out.

Meanwhile, the kids in the audience were bawling. They were terrified and couldn't stop crying. Someone behind a curtain was getting murdered, and God was somehow involved. Parents and helpers rushed around the room, trying in vain to calm everyone down. The whole event concluded with an altar call to accept Chain Saw Jesus into your life.

This is a tricky topic to write on because we're told to fear the Lord, and there's definitely fear present there. But I think events like that are why I have friends who say things like, "I'm so glad I didn't grow up in church. I became a believer when I was older, so I didn't have to unlearn much." Those kids would have accepted My Little Pony into their heart that day if it would have ended the chain saw sin massacre. The emotion they learned, the threshold they had to cross that led to God, was raw fear. He's terrifying. He wants to hurt you. He wants to cut you in half to remove your sin.

I think sometimes this happens because we want to take a shortcut to salvation for someone. We want them to be saved right this second and right this moment, and love can feel like it's taking too long. Love is messy and slow. It unravels at God's speed, not ours. Shame is faster. Fear is faster. And if the goal is to get them in the door, then fear becomes a pretty good method.

To tell you the truth, terrifying someone into a relationship with God is also easier. Love makes us vulnerable. I have to throw myself out there and be honest and naked and open to getting rejected if love is what I give to you. But fear doesn't require any of that. I can yell and scream and try to intimidate you without getting hurt or taking any real risks. Love is harder because it demands that I get personally involved in your life. Fear doesn't carry those same requirements.

But it does come with things like chain saws. That's probably the other reason we try to scare people into a relationship with Jesus. Fear has better props than love, whose primary prop is a twirling ribbon. Look it up, it's true.

THE BIBLE

When I was in college, I heard a classmate sing a great song at church. Later that week in the cafeteria, I asked him if he wrote it. Without missing a beat he replied, "No, God did." Then he walked away. He should have punctuated that answer with "You sweaty heathen" because that's how I felt. And come on, the song wasn't *that* good. The Bible, sure, that's God's book, but that John Mayer-ish worship song? God probably didn't even like the chorus, never mind write the whole thing.

SUDDENLY REALIZING YOU OWN FOURTEEN BIBLES

No one ever sets out to own fourteen Bibles. This is not a goal anyone commits to paper and tucks inside their wallet so that they can constantly remind themselves, "Someday, I'm going to own my bodyweight in Bibles!" No one hoards Bibles like a squirrel on purpose or smuggles them out of church in their pants legs. We never intend for this to happen, and yet somewhere along the way, in your Christian walk, you're going to wake up one day and say, "Whoa, I own fourteen Bibles."

It all starts off innocently; everyone needs a Bible, so you buy one. And you like it, it's nice, but you didn't realize how many options there were. You were expecting to go to the store and say, "I'd like to buy a Bible," and have the guy behind the counter who probably would have a mustache and overalls and look vaguely like a character from a Norman Rockwell painting say, "Sure, got a fresh shipment in last night. Looks like it's goin' to be a cold winter; muskrats are running. Here you go. Enjoy your Bible." But that's not how it happened at all, is it?

When you showed up to the store they pointed you to the Bible section. The section! There are rows and rows of Bibles. You had no idea there were so many varieties. And so you started looking through them but it's overwhelming. Authorized Version? Who authorized it? What does that mean? Are the rest of the Bibles considered unauthorized? Like that biography of Ralph Macchio you read? Holman Christian Standard? Who's Holman? How come he gets to set the standard? And what does Douay-Rheims mean? That's fun to say, kind of like your favorite phrase, "nougat bungalow," but what does that mean?

So you pace the aisles and try to find a *Stuff Christians Like* version, but there's not one ... yet.

And then you just buy one. In a sweaty huff you buy one and for a while it's okay. But then you see your friend's Bible. Then you read some other versions and you think, "I bought the wrong one. I need to get a new one." So you go back to the store months later, and you buy the one you like. Now you've got two, your first Bible, which is special for sentimental reasons, and your second Bible, which is now your "I'm going to read this one daily" version.

It's great too. You love that Bible, but it's awful heavy. Have you noticed that? Carrying it on trips is no fun, lugging it around church is kind of a hassle, and forget about putting it in your purse. It's like putting volume "K" of the encyclopedia in there. Maybe you should get one that's streamlined. Something small and compact and portable. Maybe with a magnet clasp. That would be a lot easier wouldn't it? Now you're up to three.

Then a holiday rolls around and your family members or friends that aren't Christians think, "What should we get him for Christmas or his birthday? What do you buy a Christian? How about a Bible? Christians love Bibles." So you get one as a gift. Now you've got four.

Which isn't too many; four Bibles isn't obscene. But then you start a new Bible study group and you're going to read through Proverbs. It sure would be nice to write in your Bible, to take some notes and write in the margins, but the Bible you use has margins that are approximately .01 inches wide. You would have to possess the precision of a Japanese blowfish chef to write in that Bible. And hey, look at this, there's a new journaling Bible with notebook lines built right in. Welcome to Bible number five.

Five is good. We're done at five. If we ever had to play a game of basketball against the Koran, we would be able to suit up an entire team. That's enough. But then a friend comes over and lo and behold you get to witness to them. You're not even sure how that happened, but right there in your living room you're telling them about how much God loves them. And they don't own a Bible. You've got to give them a Bible; everyone needs a Bible. So you give them number two from your lineup and you have to go back to the store. Hmmm, what if that happens again? What if you're the next John the Baptist and you're on some kind of streak? How many houses are in your cul-de-sac? Eight. There are eight people who live near you who might need Bibles at some point. Now you've got twelve.

But what if they don't come to you? What if you have to go to them? What if you're visiting them and they bring up God? Better get a spare Bible to keep in your car, a "car Bible" if you will. Now you've got thirteen.

And you're not superstitious. Numbers don't hold power over you. Sure seven is holy and six is evil, but thirteen isn't unlucky. That's just silly, and yet at the same time it doesn't seem wise to own thirteen Bibles. And so you return to the store ...

DOMINATING THE "PLEASE TURN TO ..." BIBLE RACE DURING CHURCH

I'm one of the fastest Bible verse finders on the East Coast of the United States of America.

Go ahead and laugh. While you're chuckling, I'll be in James 5:10 or Psalm 119:4 or Matthew 4:2. You don't know where I'm headed. I'm like a hurricane of fingers and verses and underlining. It's a thing of beauty, really. The moment the minister tells us to turn to a verse, I'm like a cheetah shot out of a cannon from the backseat of a Ferrari. I'm that fast.

In violation of the covenants of the STG (Speed Turner's Guild), I'm going to reveal some of the secrets to consistently winning the "please turn to ..." Bible race. Sure, reading the Bible is about learning from God's Word, but it's also about beating the person you're sitting with. God hates silver medals. (That's somewhere in the Bible.)

The Mint Approach

Eventually it becomes easy to tell when a minister is about to say those magical words, "Please turn to." When you recognize it's about to happen, start slowing down the people around you. A great way is to simply ask for a mint or a piece of gum right before the minister gives the command. While they're fumbling with Orbit Maui Melon Mint gum, you'll already be well on your way to finding the verse.

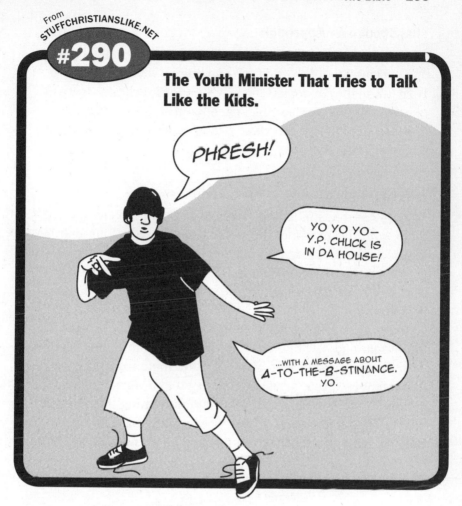

The Message Approach

This one is a little more deceptive, but such is the life of a speed turner. Replace your friend's Bible with a copy of *The Message* the night before. It doesn't list any verse numbers. It just says John 10, not John 10:10. They might beat you to the chapter, but once they do, they'll find themselves staggering in a swamp of modern translation with no specific address. Victory!

The Stockpile Approach

You have to be subtle about this one. In the moments leading up to "please turn to," ask if you can borrow your friend's Bible. Then, when they're not looking, put it under your chair. Now ask to borrow someone else's Bible and keep repeating that move. A skilled practitioner can clear a four- or five-person radius of Bibles in under a minute.

The Knockdown Approach

Juvenile? Perhaps. Effective? Without a doubt. Simply slap the Bible from the hands of the person next to you. This one is frowned upon because it's "dishonorable," but then so is asking for a piece of gum when used as a distraction tactic. Do you want to win, or do you want to love your neighbor? Oh, you want to love your neighbor?

There are other methods, but I have to keep a few secrets for myself. And now that churches are putting the verse up on video screens, this is kind of a dying art. There's one last thing to remember: If your minister is engaged in a yearlong sermon series on the book of Acts, don't bother playing the "please turn to" game. Everyone knows where the passages are. It's like dunking a basketball on a little kid. There's no pride in that.

WONDERING WHETHER THE OLD TESTAMENT STILL COUNTS

Could we get a ruling about whether the Old Testament is still in play? Seriously, could we get some sort of official with a wise-looking beard to once and for all say, "The Old Testament still counts"?

We don't have that yet, which means every now and then I'll quote something from the Old Testament and a friend will go,

"Yeah, but that's Old Testament. That's old covenant. Jesus changed all that. Your argument doesn't hold up."

I'll slink off, kind of embarrassed and disappointed. "Dang it! I keep forgetting the Old Testament's not official anymore, which is a shame because it's really long. I hate to just throw out that whole section of the Bible."

Which is silly. No one would ever say the whole Old Testament doesn't count. Clearly, Psalms is still in. Everyone loves Psalms. And Proverbs. You don't even have to be a Christian to love Proverbs — it's just so full of great wisdom. And most of the really fun stories are in the Old Testament. No one wants to get rid of Jonah and the whale or David and Goliath. And who doesn't like to hear a minister occasionally preach some crazy, funkified sermon on the Song of Solomon?

THAT GUY WHO CAN ALWAYS FIND A BIBLE VERSE THAT SAYS THE OPPOSITE OF YOURS

I wasn't a very fun person to trade baseball cards with when I was a kid. I was great at building forts and throwing acorns and playing Frisbee, but when it came to baseball cards, I was a card value jerk. When someone wanted to trade, I'd get out my dog-eared magazine that listed the current estimated prices of all the cards. Then I'd say things like, "I don't know about trading Bobby Bonilla for Mark McGwire. It says here that Bobby Bonilla is worth fifteen cents more." And if the numbers didn't line up, I didn't want to do business with you. Eventually people stopped trading cards with me.

Some Christians like to take that approach to Bible reading. They don't read God's Word to learn or grow or have their faith challenged — they read it to prove that you're wrong. It's uncanny. You almost start to wonder if they aren't standing outside your windows in the bushes at night, jotting down any verses they see you reading. Because no matter what it is you say, they've got three counterpoints and are more than happy to show you how wrong you are, both from an Old Testament point of view as well as from the New Testament. This person tends to come in three varieties:

Obscure Translator

There are approximately 970 types of Bibles, and somehow the obscure translator owns them all. Even if you do all your homework. Even if you've checked out the NIV, the ESV, and the KJV, as soon as you open your mouth, the obscure translator is going to mentally start going through their rolodex of Bible translations and say, "You're wrong, because in Gutenberg's original copy of the Bible, that verse is written differently."

Out-of-Context Dude

It's pretty easy to make the Bible say a lot of things when you rip single verses or examples right out of context. You can grab one verse, plaster it on a sign, and march to your heart's content, portraying God as someone who's really excited that people are going to hell. This is exactly what Out-of-Context Dude, or OCD, likes to do. I once wrote about the importance of accountability partners on my blog. A reader responded with something like, "Yeah, well what about Joseph? He didn't have an accountability partner, did he?" Wow, I thought ... you got me.

Generalizer

If someone ever says to you, "Didn't Paul say ..." then beware, my friend, you might be near a Generalizer. The Generalizer is the lazy version of the OCD. He doesn't have any specific examples from the Bible, and asking for an "address" on the verse he's referencing is not going to get you anywhere. Instead, expect some wide sweeping comments like, "I think Jesus said," or "One time Moses ..." or "In the New Testament

..." It's a brilliant stroke actually, because you can't prove them wrong. Think about it. If someone says, "Somewhere in the Old Testament it says, 'Life is not simple,'" you're not going to check the entire Old Testament to prove them wrong.

Ultimately, I've given up trying to beat these people. They don't want to talk Bible; they want to win. And the Bible isn't a competition. It's God's Word. Unless you're at a Bible quiz event, which is indeed a competition.

NOT THROWING AWAY A BIBLE

You can't throw away a Bible. That's the Christian equivalent of changing your own oil and then just dumping the old sludge in the street. And lighting it on fire and then flipping off anyone who comes over to see what the blaze is all about. I probably just under-exaggerated that analogy. That's how much God doesn't like it when we throw away our Bibles.

But Bibles break. Even really nice Bibles eventually fall apart if you use them enough. The binding comes undone. The glue that holds everything together gets brittle and old. Or maybe you just bought the wrong version. Maybe you wanted a different translation but liked the cover design and picked up a Bible, thinking, "I really like the color. I'm sure the translation will be fine." But it's not. It's not fine at all. So now you have a Bible you don't really want, but you can't return it to the store. If you did, you'd be the guy who says, "Yeah, this thing didn't 'take.' I'd like to get my money back, please."

What to do? What to do? You have more options than you think.

Make it a "show Bible."
Instead of throwing it away, retire your Bible to the mantel in your house. If it's worn down and beaten-up looking, people will naturally assume it's because you've been studying it so much,

as opposed to, say, keeping it in the trunk of your car next to your tire iron. Everyone who sees it will think, "Wow, she loves the Bible." If you don't have a mantel, a bookshelf will work just as well, as long as your Show Bible isn't spooning with your collection of romance novels.

Let it ride shotgun with the Gideon Bible.

Open the drawer of most hotel rooms around the world and you're likely to find a copy of the Bible. The Gideon's International organization passes them out, which is awesome. But often, their green or brown Bible is sitting in there all alone with only the occasional phone book or a "Here's-where-the-buffet-restaurants-in-town-are-located" brochure for company. Give that Gideon a running mate by adding your Bible. Maybe yours is the version the next hotel guest would actually prefer. Maybe you'll get a new ministry, praying for the people who stay in Room 412 in the Cleveland, Ohio, Ramada Inn. At the bare minimum, it would be pretty cool to see lots of people start jam-packing hotel bedside tables with Bibles. Imagine if you could barely open the drawer because it was so heavy with Bibles people had donated.

Give it away.

Sometimes, you see an immediate need and have to give your Bible to someone right away. God says, "Yeah, this person needs my Word, right now, right here. Let's do this thing." And so you have to gut your Bible on the fly, dumping out any bulletins, sermon notes, and other random slips of paper as fast as you can. Then you hand the Bible to that person and think quietly to yourself, "I hope I didn't write anything in the margin like my prayer that God would remove my heart of hate against you."

JUDGING PEOPLE WHO USE THE TABLE OF CONTENTS IN THEIR BIBLE

Stop, just stop, it's too late. I saw you. We were just told to turn to Nahum 2:4 by our pastor and out of the corner of my eye I saw you flip to the table of contents in your Bible.

Don't, don't try to explain yourself. I thought you loved God. I thought that when we weren't at church together you were off somewhere reading your Bible, but clearly that was a mistake on my part. How long has this been going on, this, ugh, I don't even like how the words feel in my mouth, this "using the table of contents to find books of the Bible"?

Do you know what I did with my table of contents? I ripped it out and rolled it into a homemade shofar horn that I blow when it's time for my family to come down and read our nightly Bible studies.

I felt like we had made so much progress. When we first met, you had a Bible with those indents, those "dumb thumbs." As in, "I'm dumb, I can't find Titus, here is where I place my thumb." But we got through that, we pushed through and got you a grown-up Bible without indents marking the different books.

And then today, today I catch you using the table of contents? Who are you?

I don't even know you any more.

Sure, you can find Psalms. Congratulations, you know where Psalms is. Everyone can find that book. It's sixty pages long and in the middle. Yeah, that's right, in addition to the location of the books of the Bible I know the length of each book.

Go on, look up Nahum. It's too late to save face now. You'll find it on page 1466 and it's only seven pages long. But what am I telling you for? You've probably confused Nahum with the Marvel comics anti-hero, Namor the Sub-Mariner, prince of Atlantis, grandson of the Atlantean Emperor Thakorr.

I'm so embarrassed for you.

THE GOD WAD

I hate having things in my pockets. When I sit down in church, I immediately empty everything I'm carrying onto the floor in front of me, creating an obstacle course of pens and keys and mints for anyone unfortunate enough to scoot by me. But one thing I love carrying is my "God Wad."

The God Wad (or Wad o' God if you prefer names with an o' in them) is exactly what it sounds like. It's a collection of 3x5 note cards I carry around with Bible verses on them. You can usually judge the health of my walk by the girth of the wad. If I'm spending lots of time in God's Word, expect to see a God Wad that's a few inches thick. If I'm slacking, my pockets will be riding empty.

I've carried some of the verses, like the official "worrier's prayer," Philippians 4:6–7, so long that the note cards feel worn and leathery. Others, like Romans 5:5, are new and fresh and still haven't gotten broken in when I've pulled the verse out in the middle of a tense moment and said, "Yikes, I'm going to need some extra God Wad today."

In three years of carrying them, I've only given one verse out. A Somalian woman who was cutting my hair opened up to me about what it felt like to be a refugee, and I felt like God wanted me to share a bit of the wad. So I did. I had written a new card that morning and handed it to her after my haircut. When I went back the next time to get my haircut she was ecstatic about how dead-on that verse was for her situation. I thought to myself, "I knew that when I wrote that verse down in the morning to add it to my God Wad, there would be a Somalian woman I'd never met before who probably needed it. I'm so wise."

I didn't think that, actually. I was just glad I had some pocket God to share with her. And that's how the God Wad tends to work. You never know when you're going to need it or who it's for. I walked out of a meeting one day at work and saw some of my God Wad sitting on a filing cabinet. I must have dropped the note cards during the day. I felt a little like Johnny Appleseed, but I quickly picked them up and said to myself, "If you love something, set it free. If it comes back to you, then it loves you too. You really love me, God Wad. You really do."

My plan is that if more people than just my mom buy this book and I become a Christian Thousandaire, I'm going to buy a laminator. Then, I'll laminate my God Wad and be able to carry it forever.

Dare to dream, Jonathan Acuff. Dare to dream.

PARENTS

On most Friday nights we take our kids to the pet store or "the free zoo." My three-year-old daughter likes to touch all the lizard tanks and the rat cages and then put her hands in her mouth. I used to pride myself on my hand sanitizing skills, but one night while driving home from the pet store, I looked in the rearview mirror and saw that she had removed her sandals and was enthusiastically licking the bottom of them. Awesome.

GETTING DRAGGED OUT OF SERVICE WHEN YOUR KID GETS KICKED OUT OF SUNDAY SCHOOL

When you hear your name called on the television game show *The Price Is Right*, that's a good thing. It means you're about to go bid on fantastic prizes and possibly spin a giant wheel to win a motor home and a Corvette or a croquet set and three lawn chairs. Jumping up and down and yelling with excitement is an appropriate response. But you shouldn't do that if you're getting called out in the middle of church to go pick up your kid from Sunday school.

At most churches they won't call out your name during the service. If the church is small enough, they'll send a Sunday school volunteer to come find you and let you know that you've won a screaming, inconsolable child. At my church, they flash a number up on a screen that corresponds with the laminated tag you got when you dropped off your child. There, in the middle of the sermon, in two-foot-high type, you'll see, "Child #413 in Room #218."

I have to admit, as soon as I see a number called on screen, I do two things immediately. I look at my own cards to make sure it's not my kids. Then, with a sense of relief at finding out it's not, I scan the room to see who just got the hook. Even with thousands of people in the crowd, I anxiously scrutinize the seated heads, watching for that one person who stands up. Oh, there you are. You lost the kid lottery. But how are you going to handle the walk of shame?

I think there are two appropriate ways to pull it off successfully.

Denial

Pretend you got a cell phone call. As soon as you see your number come up on the screen, put your cell phone against your ear, point to it, and make that face that says, "Excuse me, I need to take this call. Very important call, very important call. Has nothing to do with the screaming kid in room #218. Weird coincidence. That kid must be some sort of monster. Probably has horrible parents." If you want to go an extra step, actually pretend you're having a conversation on the phone, whispering things like, "You need me to volunteer at the homeless shelter again? *Right now?* Okay. I'm on my way." In addition to tricking people into thinking it's not your kid, you can earn some extra holy points as well.

The Double-Arm Shrug

This move has been perfected by parents with screaming kids on airplanes the world over. As soon as you see your number come up, you stand and do a double-arm shrug as if to say, "Kids will be kids." Smile and point to your watch. "It's like clockwork. Same time every Sunday." It works even better if you have a little audio file on your cell phone that plays that "waaaa whaaaa" defeated trumpet sound they play in cartoons when the Road Runner drops an anvil on the Coyote.

I haven't been called out of church (yet) to pick up one of my kids from Sunday school, but my day is coming. My daughter L.E. recently got her first stitches—in the chin of course—my daughter McRae inspired that phone call to Poison Control, and we had our first homework sent back incomplete from the teacher. It's a magical time of firsts at the Acuff house right now. And when my number does come up, please expect to see me walking briskly through the aisles during service whispering into my cupped hand, "How many orphans? Of course. I'll be right there."

FEELING COMPELLED TO TELL SUNDAY SCHOOL TEACHERS WHY YOUR KID HAS BEEN ABSENT THE LAST FEW WEEKS

Whenever we miss a few weeks of church, I feel compelled to explain the absence to my daughter's Sunday school teacher or anyone else who will listen for that matter.

If we've been out of town for a few weekends in a row, I'll make sure to use some not-so-subtle sentences that tell the teacher where we've been when I drop off my daughter at the door. "Here's L.E. She can't wait to tell you about the beach." Or, "L.E. is excited about Sunday school and wants to share all about her trip to the mountains, where we were last week, and not worshipping satan somewhere if that's what you assumed by our absence."

Why do I do that? Part of the reason is that at our church, there are so many kids that they have to carefully assign headcount to certain rooms. And there's a big chart of sticker nametags hanging on the door. If you miss too many weeks, they remove your kid's name from the wall. Like that scene in *Back to the Future* where Michael J. Fox disappears from the photo, your kid no longer exists in that room.

It doesn't stop with Sunday school though. I'll catch myself trying to explain why we missed church to random people who happen to sit in our same section week after week. I don't know their last names, but I still feel compelled to let them know we had perfectly legitimate reasons not to be at church for a few weeks.

Maybe it's a pastor's kid thing. Church is what we did every Sunday morning. Not attending was out of the question. That would have been like giving both God and my dad the middle finger, so we went. Maybe it's a fear thing too. I think people who are regular church attendees have a closer relationship with God, and in case I ever come up in their conversations with him, I want to make sure they have the most accurate attendance information and can pass on my excuses directly to him. Or maybe I think God is up there with a checklist like Santa Claus, and when he sees me miss church, that's a huge black mark.

It's probably a potpourri of all three things, which stinks a little, but I'll work it out next week, at church. Which is where I'll be. If God asks you, please let him know I'm going pretty regularly. Except when we're at the beach.

SPRINTING TO YOUR CAR AFTER CHURCH

I love my in-laws. They're great people. I'll be honest with you though: They're dead weight when it comes to the after-church car sprint. I didn't realize this until one Sunday morning when they slowed us down on the dash to get our kids from Sunday school and make it home as fast as possible.

I was happy to sit with them during church. But when we were dismissed at the end of service, I needed them to be like remoras, riding along with me as I progressed shark-like through the masses. Instead, they were like tugboats or anchors or whatever nautical device means "slow."

For their sake, and anyone else who needs a refresher on getting to your car quickly after church, here are a few simple tips:

Stretch during the final prayer.

I can't say this enough, people. You've just spent up to an hour sitting. Your muscles are going to be tight and not ready for speed. So when the minister asks you to bow your head, please do, but keep right on going over and touch your toes. Stretch your calves. Loosen up your joints. If you do it the right way, not only will you get in a good stretch, but people will probably think you're really spiritual.

Sit at the end of the aisle.

The last thing you want is to be sitting next to a "gatherer." Gatherers are always surprised church is over despite the fact that it ends the same time every Sunday, all year long. They slowly pick up every item they brought with them ... one ... by ... one. "Let's see ... Here's my Bible. And there's my bulletin. Now let me grab my pen. And my cough drops. And my little journal for sermon notes. Here are my keys. Oh, look! They fell off the key ring onto the floor. Here's my house key. Here's my car key ..." You need to sit on the end of the aisle so that you can burst out of the seat like an Olympic sprinter coming off the blocks.

Tinkle at home or your next destination.

I wish that word was not in my vernacular, but there it is. I have little kids, so that word's here to stay for at least a few years. What's *not* here to stay is me and my kids in the church bathroom. Every minute you stay there equates to minutes you could be doing something else. So either train them to use the bathroom during Sunday school—that's on their time—or convince them to use the bathroom at home or at Walmart. That way, they won't get mesmerized by the uniqueness of the away game at church and take ten extra minutes. And you'll get to your car a lot faster.

COLLECTIVELY DECIDING THAT THE PHRASE "SUNDAY SCHOOL" IS HORRIBLE, OLD-FASHIONED, AND PERHAPS SYNONYMOUS WITH SOME SORT OF RELIGIOUS DUNGEON

Did we take a vote? Nobody ever tells me anything. I swear, you take a few years off and when you come back to church, the phrase "Sunday school" is getting pummeled like a piñata full of Harry Potter books. We have to call it "Group Time Discussion" or "Happenings" or "Lifetime" or a million other words that essentially mean "the time you meet together on Sunday and talk about the Bible and life in a classroom-type environment." Or in other words: Sunday school.

But I'm cool with that. I promise I am. I've often heard that when the phrase "estate tax" was changed to "death tax," voters started caring about the issue, because previously they thought the estate tax only applied to rich people. And maybe it's like that—if you tell a first-time visitor where Sunday school is, they'll immediately slap you in the mouth and get back in their car. But if you say "small group," they're okay and will probably become lifetime members that Sunday.

Just promise me that we won't correct people that still roll retro and call it Sunday school. That happened to a friend of mine who said her three-year-old really enjoyed Sunday school. "Oh," a woman in the church hallway said, "You mean small group?" Sure. Small group. The three-year-old is going to pick up on a subtle difference in the vernacular. Her parents mailed her pacifier to Cinderella when she needed to kick the habit, but the name nuance is going to matter to her. Sure.

FEEDING KIDS THEIR BODY WEIGHT IN GOLDFISH CRACKERS

Years from now when my kids are older, they'll probably think of Jesus whenever they even smell a Goldfish cracker. I'm sure this is a kid thing, not just a Christian thing, but on about fifty-one Sundays of the year, that's what they have for snack. And at our church, if your kid cries a ton, before they flash their number on the video screen in the sanctuary asking you to come get them, they put them in a wagon, pull them around, and stuff them full of Goldfish. It's like this little red wagoned parade of wailing in the halls. Eyes streaming tears, mouth full of fish, tiny hands clutching the side of the "Bye Bye Buggy," counting the minutes until a parent can come rescue them. Good times.

MISSIONAL POSTMODERN RELEVANCE

I'm not really sure what those three words mean anymore, but my friends who are cooler than me and have nicer hair use them all the time. Seriously, they'll call breakfast sausages "postmodern" if the mood strikes them right. So I thought if I combined all three words into one catch-all section of miscellaneous essays, the combined power would be unstoppable, like if the Ninjas Snake Eyes and Storm Shadow from GI Joe formed a band with Terence Trent D'Arby. That last sentence was straight up Missional Postmodern Relevance at its finest.

KEEPING MISSION TRIP SANDALS AS PROOF YOU'VE BEEN TO AFRICA

Now clearly, the idea of buying a souvenir while in a foreign country is not something unique to Christians. Everyone who travels does that. What's unique is the belief that these items will serve as a symbol of our trip, a celebration of the culture we experienced, and a constant reminder of how God moved and the Holy Spirit was present and lives were changed in powerful, everlasting ways. Which honestly, is an awful lot to ask of a pair of rubber sandals.

What usually happens is that about a week after you get home, you put those things in a box under your bed. But I thought it would be interesting to take a quick walk down mission trip memory lane, get that box out, and see what we've all put into it.

Art

Nothing says "I went on a mission trip" like a piece of tribal art hanging on the living room wall. It doesn't matter that 98 percent of the house is decorated in rustic Americana antiques. There, in all its glory, is a dark wooden mask or giraffe statue proudly saying, "Yeah, that's right—it's a giraffe. The rest of the house looks like Martha Stewart, but I don't even care. I had to wrap this thing in dirty clothes and cradle it gently in my suitcase to even get it home without breaking it. You'd better believe this is hanging on my wall." Eventually the husband or wife who didn't go on the mission trip will move this art to a less popular room in your house, then to the guest bathroom, and eventually to your garage. This is the migratory path most mission trip art travels.

The bowl or basket

I love these. Occasionally, you'll go to a friend's house for dinner, and one of the items they serve will be in an oddly shaped bowl you've never seen before. "Oh, this?" they'll say casually. "We spent some time abroad on a mission trip." And although it's a lovely bowl or basket holding bread, you know all the other dishes in the cabinets hate it. "Look at that bowl. Handmade, brought from thousands of miles away. 'I'm so fancy. Look at me and my earthen details. I have to be hand-washed. Don't drop me. I'm delicate.' Punk bowl." (Your cookware doesn't talk? You don't do this in your head? You should.)

Sandals

When my youth group went to an island in the Lesser Antilles— such a delightful phrase to say!—we all got some rainbow-colored, hard plastic sandals. I'm not sure that I've ever owned any other clothing item that was rainbow and hard plastic, but for those two weeks, I refused to wear anything else on my feet. We loved those sandals and were convinced we would be wearing them the entire summer. But for some reason, what works well on an island in the Caribbean doesn't work quite as well in central Massachusetts. They got put into a box pretty quickly, but I swear if I still had them, I'd bust them out now, if only to frighten the much softer, much more comfortable Crocs I see everywhere.

Weapons

As a sophomore in high school, I didn't have a whole lot of access to swords. Until I went on mission trips, that is. Suddenly, it was completely okay for me to buy a two-foot-long machete. What would have been confiscated by my parents if I brought it home from the hardware store down the street was suddenly cultural, even religious, because I bought it on a mission trip. Did I still accidentally cut myself with it and practice throwing it into the ground like some sort of adventurer with acne? Without a doubt.

And if your question is, "Is it true that when your wife goes out of town you carry around the Maasai warrior club your brother got you from Kenya for protection against the cat burglars you feel are lurking in your very safe, very quiet suburban neighborhood?" the answer is yes. But only because I'm a wuss with an active imagination.

FAKE LAUGHING AT UNFUNNY JOKES OUT OF CHRISTIAN LOVE

We're supposed to do this, right?

As Christians, the compassionate, Christlike thing to do when someone says something unfunny is to pretend it is funny and fake laugh your head off, right?

Or maybe what we're supposed to do is be the truth in this situation. To not lie, and to honestly say, "I have to confess, my Christian brother, your joke about chili is not funny, and I've heard you say it seventeen times since I joined this small group, and it has progressively gotten less funny with each telling, which I did not anticipate being possible when I heard it the first time."

It's quite the pickle. I'm unaware of a scene in the Bible that gives us clear direction on this problem. I can't recall Jesus ever saying to Andrew, "I forgive you, but I can't abide by the lack of humor found in your 'Why'd the rooster crow three times? 'Cause Peter crossed the road' joke. That's not funny."

But even though Jesus might not have addressed joke quality head on, I do think you can make a case both for and against fake laughing using some of the fruits of the spirit in Galatians 5:

Fruit of the Spirit: Love

You should always fake laugh.

Who are you to judge what's funny and not funny? Give someone your fake laugh out of love, like the math teachers who used to give me an "A for effort." Did I suck at math? You bet I did. But I tried. So did your friend. Bad joke or not, fake laugh out of love.

You should never fake laugh.

As a Christian, you've got to reflect loving truth back to people. What if your husband tells you an unfunny joke at home, you fake laugh, he thinks it's funny, and then he tells all his friends later and they don't laugh. He's embarrassed, you've denied him a "joke improvement opportunity," or JIO as we call it at the Acuff house, and all his friends had to experience something unfunny. Everyone loses in that situation. Don't fake laugh.

Fruit of the Spirit: Peace

You should always fake laugh.

It was a passing comment. It was a quick joke and the conversation has already moved on. Let it go. It walked into the room briefly, fell on a banana peel of unfunny, and was dragged back into the "closet of no laughter" before you even had to stare at it for very long. Keep the peace. Fake laugh.

You should never fake laugh.

"Oh, was that a joke?" is the worst thing you can hear someone say after you've unleashed what you thought was hilarious.

("You're fired" is actually worse, but the first one happens far more often.) Help your friends so they never hear this question. Be honest with each other. Don't fake laugh.

Fruit of the Spirit: Patience

You should always fake laugh.

They're going to get funny. They'll get better. Have patience, have patience, don't be in such a hurry. (You just got Psaltyed, which is what I'm now saying instead of "You just got served!" Oh, the irony of an unfunny, obscure joke in the middle of an essay about unfunny jokes. I'm going to rip the fabric of time if I'm not careful here.) Trust in the Lord and he'll renew your friend's mind and sense of humor. Have patience. Fake laugh.

You should never fake laugh.

Life is very, very short. The only day we're given is the one we've got. Every rose has its thorn. (Poison lyrics? Really?) In marriage, they say never go to bed angry. Same logic applies here. Don't let the sun go down on something unfunny. Be patient in how you break the news to them, but don't let another moment go by that could be funnier if you were only a little more honest.

Fruit of the Spirit: Self-Control

You should always fake laugh.

If you can't actually bring yourself to guffaw out loud, at least have the self-control to say what fake laughers the world over say when they don't want to hurt someone's feelings: "That's funny." If anyone ever says that to you, they didn't think what you just said was funny, because if they did, they would have just laughed instead. Since most people don't realize that, show self-control and gentleness and all the other fruits of the spirit and say, "That's funny." Fake laugh.

You should never fake laugh.

Sarah didn't fake laugh when she heard the Lord tell Abraham they were going to have a kid even though they were both in their nineties. She laughed out loud in Genesis 18:12 and got busted by God in perhaps what is my favorite random scene in the Bible:

Sarah: I did not laugh.

God: Yes, you did laugh.

Is that what you want to happen when you get to heaven? God reviews a highlight film of your life that shows you fake laughing over and over again while you just shake your head and say, "I didn't fake laugh." And he says, "Oh you fake laughed, you did fake laugh." Don't ever fake laugh.

THE SMELL OF OLD HYMNALS

Chances are, when you read the title of this essay, you knew exactly what I was talking about. That odd bouquet of faded red or blue hymnals, old yellowed paper, and slight undertones of hand sweat. That's because smell is the strongest sense associated with memory.

I miss that hymnal smell. It's what church smells like to me. Worship music splashed on video screens doesn't have a scent. Even a good song like "How Great Is Our God" won't create a memory that transports me back to that time when I was a kid and the hymnal was heavy and my heart was light.

If I get rich and famous, please know that I will create a cologne and a perfume that smell like old hymnals. (The perfume will be called "For Hymnal.") Girls can wear it if they want to marry a pastor. Guys can wear it if they want to meet a nice Christian girl with a good, old-school church upbringing.

In the meantime, I think I'm going to find a small church and roll around in a bunch of hymnals when no one is looking, like Scrooge McDuck in his money vault. I'll probably take one too and hang it from the rearview mirror of my car.

INTERPRETIVE DANCE / MIMING

I took a break dancing class when I was in the third grade in Ipswich, Massachusetts. I know what you're thinking: "Of course you did. You were growing up on the mean streets of a New England beach community. Breakin' was the only voice you had to express the soul-crushing hardships of being middle class."

In high school I took tap dancing and ballroom dancing. I know what you're thinking: "Of course you did. Nothing says 'I'm super popular' like strapping on a pair of tap shoes and speaking to the world with the pitter patter of your feet."

In college I took swing dancing. I know what you're thinking: "Hey, we all went through a Brian Setzer stage. We all got caught up in the swing craze for about fifteen minutes in 1998. That was a crazy time."

Now, as I stare down a topic that a wheelbarrow full of people have emailed me about, I just can't do it. I can't lay into interpretive dance. I like dancing too much. It's ingrained in who I am, and given the chance, I'd probably be on stage jumping around to a contemporary worship song with a ribbon. I can't make fun of it. That said, I can laugh about mime. In fact, I'm pretty sure even God laughs at that a little.

There's something about painting your face, wearing all black except for white gloves, and pretending you can't speak that's simply hysterical. It's like some sort of fine potpourri of comedy. Even when it's outside of church, it's pretty funny. But Christianity + Mime = Awesome.

A friend of mine went to a women's Bible study once. One of the members said that she had something God had laid on her heart that she had to do. After disappearing for a few minutes, she emerged from the bathroom in full mime regalia. She then proceeded to perform a mime version of the crucifixion of Christ. (There's nothing funny about the crucifixion of Christ, so if you just laughed a little, you should feel pretty ashamed of yourself.) She carried an imaginary cross, was nailed up, and because by mime law you have to do this, performed the invisible box move where you pretend you're trapped inside a box no one else can see. Of course the box was the tomb and the mime was Jesus, but that's beside the point.

The point is that miming is funny. It's okay to laugh with it. And really, what's a mime going to do to you anyway? Of all the groups I'm afraid of angering with this book, mimes are pretty low on the list. Will they come to a book signing and throw that invisible rope on me? Are they going to give me a middle finger–based book review on the side of the street as I walk by? I have nothing to fear. If they did step to me, I'd bust out some pop 'n' lock and challenge them to a break-off. And even if they won, they can't talk. So I'd yell, "You got served!" just because I've always wanted to say that and have never really had the chance.

Of course now that I've made fun of Christian mimes, God is probably going to make me quit writing and start an inner-city mime ministry as punishment. We'll call it "Gloves of Love."

SKIPPING CHURCH IF YOU CATCH EVEN A WHIFF OF A GUEST SPEAKER

Unless I know there's going to be some sort of animal show involved—maybe called *Noah's Bark*, with a group of traveling dogs that reenact Bible stories—I'm probably going to skip the guest speaker at church.

I know I'm not the only one who does this because the parking lot and the sanctuary are significantly emptier when the senior pastor isn't there. I think my church is starting to catch on though, because they're getting pretty tricky about telling us when the senior pastor is actually going to be in the building. Using video sermons and live feeds and satellite campuses, they're shuffling him all over the place like the president during a terrorist threat. You never actually know where he is until you get there.

And sometimes you'll even get there, see him do the announcements, and then *voilà*, a guest speaker magically materializes on stage. Clearly they're on to us.

PUTTING THE DEVIL "ON NOTICE"

Have you ever heard someone do this? This might be more of a Southern Baptist thing, but I personally find it to be delightful. Here's how it typically sounds in a prayer:

"Lord, we just pray for your strength. We just lift you up, Lord. We just praise you. And devil, ohhh devil, we put you on notice. No longer will you have control over our annual bake sale. The mistakes we made last year and the fights we had at the peach pie table have been forgiven and forgotten. We put you on notice, devil."

Whenever I hear something like that I start to think about the devil. He's at home, sitting in a chair by a never ending fire of sulfur and sorrow eating a deviled egg. He's reading *The Da Vinci Code* when someone knocks at his door. He gets up, opens the door, and sees a delivery man standing there. "Uh, Mr. Devil. Just wanted to let you know that you've been put on notice. Mary Smith says you better stay away from the bake sale this year." He shrugs, walks back over to his chair, and turns on some *Jersey Shore* on MTV.

BEING VOLUNTOLD

I don't know who originally came up with the word *voluntold*, but if I did, I would side hug him for about an hour. It's such a perfect way to describe what happens when someone else forces you to volunteer for something at church or some "not random act of kindness." You haven't volunteered—someone committed you on the sly and then told you where and when to show up.

Studies I completely made up show that 84 percent of voluntold incidents originate with your parents or your spouse. You're enjoying a perfectly normal day when your mom will say, "Hey, I volunteered you to teach the next door neighbors' grandparents from China how to drive." "This can't be right," you'll think to yourself. "Did I agree to teach two sixty-year-olds how to drive? Their own kids have refused, and they're blood. Is that something I agreed to? That doesn't sound like me."

Next thing you know, you're in the passenger seat of a 1995 Honda Accord, doing impossibly slow laps around your neighborhood. For what feels like three days, you'll keep saying, "Now faster ... Now a little slower ... Watch out for that mailbox." Eventually, while still traveling 10 mph, the grandmother will throw the car directly into park in the middle of the street, causing the entire vehicle to buck into mechanical submission, and her husband will take his turn behind the wheel.

Your experience might be slightly different than mine, but I think there are three universal things you should do if you ever get voluntold:

Always pass the voluntold forward.

Spread the joy of the voluntold by taking as many people down with you as possible. I mean, "By spreading the Christian attitude of service," not "taking as many people down." That didn't come out the right way. I made my fiancée at the time ride in the back seat while I taught the elderly couple how to drive.

Tell God, "You owe me."

Find yourself doing something you didn't intend to ever sign up for? Tell God, "You owe me." Chances are he'll laugh a little and then dramatically pause and throw down: "I sent you my Son. You're watching a class of two-year-olds for one Sunday in your lifetime. Boo-yah!" I don't know if he really says Boo-yah, but it felt right.

Admit you don't want to be there.

I'm a big fan of being up front when you've been voluntold. Most of the time, if your grumpy face is screaming, "I hate cleaning dishes," but you're trying to front like you're happy to be helping out in the kitchen, people are going to know. They'll know. So be open about it. Tell the lady next to you, "My wife signed me up for this. I think God wants me to have the heart of a servant, but that hasn't happened yet. Do you have a sense of how many dishes that's going to take? Do you know how many spoons you have to wash before you get the heart of a servant? Any idea of what that number is?" Chances are they'll admit they don't love washing spoons either, and you'll become best friends and have a water fight with the soapy suds and laugh, laugh, laugh the night away.

SIDE HUGS

Yes, God wants us to be compassionate and tender with each other. Not only that, but he wants us to love our enemies and serve our neighbors. Those things are great, as long as there's no body-on-body action, such as in a "full frontal hug," one of those sinful abominations where you just wrap your arms around a friend and embrace them. That's why Christians the world over have embraced the "side hug."

In the side hug, or "A-frame" as it is also called, there's no risk of two crotches touching. Instead of face-to-face, you go side-to-side, putting your arm around the person and placing

#423

Creating the Holiest Church Logo Possible.

your hip against theirs. Still having a hard time mastering it? Pretend you're taking a photo and you're both looking at the camera together. The side hug is safe for the whole family, friendly, and above all, holy. I don't know the exact scriptural reference for it, but try the book of Psalms. That book is massive.

GETTING BAPTIZED IN THE JORDAN RIVER

We're all supposed to be equal as Christians. God is not up in heaven grading degrees of forgiven or measuring percent of awesome. Christ's death on the cross was an equal opportunity situation. If you're in, you're not kind of in or really in, you're In. Your soul is saved. Sanctification commences.

Sort of.

What we don't tell new Christians is that there is one thing you can do that kind of puts the ultimate stamp of approval on your spiritual passport. And I would do it tomorrow, but the Jordan River is a long way from Atlanta, Georgia.

I think being baptized In the Jordan River would move me in places that are currently hidden under layers of sarcasm. Maybe I'll go someday, but I'm afraid I'd throw my Jordan River status around like a verbal royal flush in my conversations with other Christians.

In any given situation, I'd find a not so subtle way to say, "That's interesting. Kind of reminds me of when I was in the Jordan River, getting baptized . . ."

Then I would just let it hang out there, to really let it sink in, that I was the only "double in" Christian. That sure, despite being baptized by the Holy Spirit, the Jordan River is where it's really at. Then God would have to strike me with lightning for my arrogance, and my wife would have to sprinkle the ashes over the Jordan River because she's a fan of irony. While they were there, my kids would get baptized in the river and become cocky too. They'd get struck by lightning eventually as well.

So I guess what I'm trying to say is that I can't get baptized in the Jordan River because my daughters would get struck by lightning. Seems pretty obvious when you think about it.

TEMPORARILY SUSPENDING OUR FAITH WHEN WE GET BEHIND THE WHEEL

Decades ago, the phrase "Sunday Driver" used to mean old ladies with big hats driving back from church at speeds thirty miles below the legal limit. Not anymore.

Sunday is now one of the most dangerous times to be on the road. If I'm headed to church and you're in my way, slowing me down and preventing me from getting a good parking spot or sitting in the same seat I always like to sit in, then get behind me satan. Or in a ditch on the side of the road—your choice. I'm fine with either.

Don't let the little fish on the back fool you. If it were up to me, when I wanted to drive all crazy I'd have a little switch in the car that would automatically transform the Jesus fish into a Darwin fish. Then people behind me would say, "That guy cut me off! Oh, he's an atheist. Phew. For a second, I thought that was the body of Christ cutting me off."

And I'll ignore you in the parking lot if I cut you off on the way to church and you then happen to park directly next to me. I'll get out of my car, stare straight ahead, and just march right into the building without ever making eye contact. I might pick up my pace a little and walk faster than normal, but that's only because I'm excited about worshipping today, not because I'm afraid of you. I don't see you. I don't see you, but God does, and he's disappointed that your cautious, within-the-law driving is keeping his sheep from returning to his flock.

THROWING THE DEVIL UNDER THE BUS FOR EVERYTHING

Sometimes I think we Christians throw satan under the bus for things he might not have been involved with. For instance, if your band at church sucks one Sunday morning, it might be really easy to say, "The enemy sure was attacking service today. None of the songs worked well, and our timing was completely off. What a mess. Satan sure was pressing in on all sides."

I agree, that's one way to look at it. Another way to look at it is that you guys didn't practice. Nobody showed up on time to rehearse the songs, and when they did, they ended up joking around, pretending they were Lincoln Brewster, or just grumbling about all the songs they'd like to play if the senior pastor would release his death grip on what's "big-church" appropriate. So when Sunday showed up, you sounded about as good as you practiced, which was awful.

Did satan do that? That's debatable. Was he down in hell watching the service saying, "Watch this: The drummer's got a completely different rhythm going and it's killing the bass player's sense of self confidence and timing. My master plan has come to fruition!" Doubtful. I think more likely he was somewhere sinking ships or punching old ladies in the kidney when a demon came and reported, "Hey, Truth Rising Baptist Church had horrible worship music today." To which he responded, "Awesome."

WRITING "XIAN" INSTEAD OF CHRISTIAN

How did this happen? I thought we were still upset that people say "X-mas" instead of "Christmas." Weren't we making bumper stickers that read, "We say Merry Christmas," to counteract the Jesus neutralization of the Christmas season? Weren't we mad that people are saying "Happy Holidays" and de-Christifying the Christmas season? I could have sworn we were. But now, I keep seeing the word "Xian" popping up to replace Christian.

Is that a postmodern thing? Did this suddenly material-ize because when you're texting or Twittering or some other technology-driven activity that will inevitably start with "T," it's easier to type "Xian"? Are we trying to save five characters? Are our fingers really that tired? Or is it an Xtreme thing? Is this an attempt to make Christ seem more relevant and hip and likely to own a snowboard?

Are we trying to Mountain Dew Christ?

SATURDAY NIGHT CRYFEST

If my publisher ever lets me go on a book tour, I'm probably going to read these essays with my prayer voice. I'll talk normally right up until we get to this section, but when we do, I'll dim the lights and throw on some mournful piano music so that I can break it down slow. You'll probably think to yourself, "Is this guy trying to make out with us?" But I'm not; I'm just trying to take these essays from your head to your heart, and every Christian knows those are the hardest twelve inches to travel.

FACEBOOK FRIEND-SUGGESTING JESUS

I will accept anyone's friend request on Facebook. I don't discriminate. I don't filter out weird people or hate on anyone that has a unibrow, like me.

But I never accept friend suggestions. If you've never used Facebook, a friend suggestion is a feature where you can send a note to someone and essentially say, "I think you should be friends with this other person." You get the other person's name and a little photo of them. If you choose to accept it, then you send that suggested person a friend request.

It's meant to be a neat little way to connect people, but I've started to get some random suggestions. Someone will send me one that says, "You should be friends with Tammy Smith, Red Bluff High School." I'll look at it, quickly realize that I don't know Tammy Smith and think, "If I accept this friend suggestion, Tammy Smith, a high school sophomore, is going to get a random friend request from a complete stranger who happens to be a thirty-four-year-old married man living in the suburbs of Atlanta with his two kids who doesn't even use his full name on Facebook and kind of has a weird smirk in his photo." Wow, the only thing missing from my induction into the creepy hall of fame

#507   The Sound Guy Neck Crane

is perhaps a mustache and a scar running down my cheek from a knife fight I got into behind a dumpster at a truck stop on the New Jersey Turnpike.

That's a completely silly thought, but while thinking about that one day, I realized that I approach witnessing to people about God in a pretty similar fashion. (I know, whoa, did he just leap from a New Jersey Turnpike knife fight story to witnessing to people about the everlasting love of Jesus Christ? Yes, yes I did.)

The truth is that sometimes I drop Jesus into someone's lap like I'm sending a random friend suggestion on Facebook. I don't really tell them much about him. I don't really invest in the life of the person I'm talking to. I don't even really listen to their story. I just rush to the end of my agenda and essentially say, "Yeah, yeah, regardless of what's going on with you and your whole situation, I'd like to send you this friend suggestion to connect with Jesus. Here you go, *vaya con Dios*, stranger."

It's kind of like a Jesus drive-by, me just spraying folks with the name of Christ and hoping it sticks. I don't think that's a particularly good thing. I can't imagine that's what God had in mind when he gave us the Great Commission. So what can we do to change that? How do we not just "friend suggest" Jesus?

I don't know. I'm all out of silver bullets, and to be honest there are about 15,000 other books that have better advice about sharing your faith. But I have started to do something differently in the last few months. I've started to ask people questions I genuinely want answers to. Instead of asking a question and then forcing the conversation back into my framework regardless of their answer, I've tried to just listen and let people talk and remain engaged in what they have to say. The more I've done that, the more I've been amazed at how willing people are to open up when you actually listen. And sometimes, when I feel like God is cool with it, I get to ask my favorite question of all, "Who is carrying all that with you?"

Because everyone has an "all that." Whether you're going through a divorce or the most wildly successful season of work in your life, everyone has an "all that" they're carrying. (Sometimes success is the most crushing "all that" you can face because what you thought would make everything perfect in your life just isn't and that's pretty terrifying.) It feels like 99 out of 100 times the answer to the question "Who is carrying all that with you?" is "no one." One woman told me she didn't want to burden her happy friends with her sadness so she keeps it hidden. One man told me he wasn't a "guy's guy" and since he didn't understand football it was hard for him to form relationships with other men.

Time after time, the answer to the question "Who is carrying all that with you?" comes back as "no one."

But it's not one of those questions you can ask and then disappear as soon as you've friend suggested Jesus. You have to be willing to carry the "all that" with the person you're talking with. You can't fade into the weeds of life like dissolving into the sea of profiles on Facebook. That's why witnessing is hard. That's why it's easier to friend suggest Jesus to strangers than it is to introduce your friend Jesus to someone.

It's not right, but I think that's why it happens. And I'm tired of it happening with me.

THINKING YOU'RE NAKED

I don't want to brag, but I'm pretty awesome at applying Band-Aids. And make no mistake, there is an art. Because if you go too quickly and unpeel them the wrong way, they stick to themselves and you end up with a wadded-up useless mess instead of the Little Mermaid–festooned bandage your daughter so desperately wants to apply to a boo-boo that may in fact be 100 percent fictional.

Half of the injuries I treat at the Acuff house are invisible or simply wounds of sympathy. My oldest daughter, L.E., will scrape her knee and my three-year-old, McRae, realizing the

Band-Aid box is open will say, "Yo Dad, I'd like to get in on that too. What do you say we put one on, I don't know, my ankle. Yeah, my ankle, let's pretend that's hurt."

But sometimes the cuts are real, like the day my five-year-old got a scrape on her face playing in the front yard. I rushed into the house and returned with a princess bandage. As I bent down to apply it to her forehead, her eyes filled up with tears and she shrank back from me.

"What's wrong?" I asked.

"I don't want to wear that Band-Aid," she replied.

"Why? You have a cut, you need a Band-Aid," I said.

"I'll look silly," she answered.

Other than her sister and her mom, there was no one else in the yard. None of her friends were over, cars were not streaming past our house and watching us play, the world was pretty empty at that moment. But for the first time I can remember, she felt shame. She had discovered shame. Somewhere, somehow, this little five-year-old had learned to be afraid of looking silly. If I were smarter, if I had been better prepared for the transition from little toddler to little girl, I might have asked her this:

"Who told you that you were silly?"

I didn't though. That question didn't bloom in my head until much later, and I didn't understand it until I saw God ask a similar question in Genesis 3:11. To me, this is one of the saddest and most profoundly beautiful verses in the entire Bible. Adam and Eve have fallen. The apple is a core. The snake has spoken. The dream appears crushed. As they hide from God under clothes they've hastily sewn together, he appears and asks them a simple question:

"Who told you that you were naked?"

There is hurt in God's voice as he asks this question, but there is also a deep sadness, the sense of a father holding a daughter that has, for the first time ever, wrapped herself in shame.

Who told you that you were not enough?

Who told you that I didn't love you?

Who told you that there was something outside of me you needed?

Who told you that you were ugly?

Who told you that your dream was foolish?

Who told you that you would never have a child?

Who told you that you would never be a father?

Who told you that you weren't a good mother?

Who told you that without a job you aren't worth anything?

Who told you that you'll never know love again?

Who told you that this was all there is?

Who told you that you were naked?

I don't know when you discovered shame. I don't know when you discovered that there were people who might think you are silly or dumb or not a good writer or a husband or a friend. I don't know what lies you've been told by other people or maybe even by yourself.

But in response to what you are hearing from everyone else, God is still asking the same question, "Who told you that you were naked?"

And he's still asking us that question because we are not.

In Christ we are not worthless.

In Christ we are not hopeless.

In Christ we are not dumb or ugly or forgotten.

In Christ we are not naked.

In Isaiah 61:10 it says, "For he has clothed me with garments of salvation and arrayed me in a robe of righteousness."

The world may try to tell you a thousand different things today. You might close this book and hear a million declarations of what you are or who you'll always be, but know this.

As unbelievable as it sounds and as much as I never expected to type this sentence in a book:

You are not naked.

CONFESSING "SAFE SINS"

Have you ever been in a small group with people who confess safe sins? Someone will say, "I need to be honest with everyone tonight. I need to have full disclosure. Like ODB from the Wu-Tang Clan, I need to give it to you raw!" So you brace yourself for this crazy moment of authenticity and the person takes a deep breath and says ... "I haven't been reading my Bible enough."

Ugh, you dirty, dirty sinner. I'm not even sure I can be in a small group with you anymore. Not reading your Bible enough, that is disgusting. And then once he's gone, someone else will catch the safe sin bug too and will say, "I need to be real too. I haven't been praying enough."

Two of you in the same room? Wow, freak shows! I can barely stand it.

But what happens when people start confessing safe sins is that everyone else in the room starts concealing their real junk. If I had been surrounded by confessions like that in the eighth grade I would have instantly known I couldn't follow the "not reading my Bible enough" guy with my own story:

"Soooo, this weekend when it was snowing I told my parents I was going to the town dump to sled, but instead I was really just digging through a 100-foot mountain of warm trash looking for pornography people had thrown away." And the same principle would have applied to me in my late twenties. I wouldn't have been honest sharing my struggles with internet porn if everyone else confessed their "safe enough for small group" sins.

And that sucks. It sucks that as broken as we all are, as desperate as we all are for a Savior, we feel compelled to clean ourselves up when we get around each other.

But writing the blog *Stuff Christians Like* has taught me something unbelievable. If I stop writing tomorrow, this will be the lesson I cling to the most.

When you go first, you give everyone in your church or your community or your small group or your blog the gift of going second.

It's so much harder to be first. No one knows what's off-limits yet and you're setting the boundaries with your words. You're throwing yourself on the honesty grenade and taking whatever fallout that comes with it. Going second is so much easier. And the ease only grows exponentially as people continue to share. But it has to be started somewhere. Someone has to go first and I think it has to be us.

Let's give the gift of going second.

FORGETTING THAT YOU ARE FAMOUS

The only time I've ever been recognized was not as weird as I thought it would be. I guess in my head I envisioned my family and I would be walking in the mall and some stranger would exclaim, "Jonathan Acuff? *The* Jonathan Acuff? Wow, it is you!" Then I would blush and maybe shield my kids behind me with my arm because this person's adoration would be so intense. They'd say, "Oh, please, say something that is both sarcastic and insightful at the same time. You're so wise and adequately heighted." I'd correct them on the use of the word "heighted," which is actually not a word, and then I'd say two or three off-the-cuff sentences that would change their life and then maybe sign their arm or a Bible if it were available. Seems like a pretty reasonable expectation, right?

It didn't happen like that. A guy just walked up to me at church and introduced himself. We talked for a few minutes about *Stuff Christians Like*. The whole thing was over before I knew it and was pretty uneventful. Which is probably exactly how God wanted it to be.

I tend to get ego drunk pretty quickly. When people compliment me, outwardly I do the Christian courtesy of immediately rejecting the kind words. Inwardly though, I'm often drinking in their kindness and doing a little "look how awesome I am" dance. I'm patting myself on the back with both arms and both legs at the same time, which is difficult but not impossible since I've taken yoga twice. (Which may or may not be "of the devil"—jury's still out on that one.)

Knowing that about myself, knowing I'm prone to massive "me parades," I am constantly wrestling with God over the unexpected growth of StuffChristiansLike.net. There's a circle of famous Christians right now: big pastors, authors who have written amazing books, speakers who stalk conference stages like cougars. And I wanted to be inside it. I wanted to become a famous Christian.

One night while jogging, I confessed that to God. As ugly and as shallow as this sounds, I said to him, "God, I want my story to give me fame. I want fame. I want to be famous."

In a split second, I felt like God laughed. Not AT me, but WITH me, which is something I feel like he regularly does. In my heart, I heard:

"Ha! You want fame? The creator of the universe knows your name. The Alpha and Omega knows who you are and what you care about. That's as famous as you're ever going to be. Whose acknowledgment of you is going to stand up next to mine?"

At that point, I started laughing too, because he was right. I'm already famous. God knew me in the womb. He knows how many hairs are on my head. He's my absolute biggest fan and I'm famous in his eyes. So are you. He's got a blog about you that is simply astounding. He follows you on Twitter and started a fan group dedicated to you on Facebook. He can't stop talking about you and pouring out love on you.

Is whatever you're doing right now in life going to make you famous? Maybe it will, maybe it won't. But ultimately it doesn't matter. As Christians, we've already peaked. We can stop worrying about trying to become famous Christians. That's done.

We are all famous.

PRETENDING WE BELIEVE ALL SINS ARE EQUAL

This one is fun to say, isn't it? You feel like you're doing something righteous just by uttering it, which is great. I'm a big fan of righteousness that involves no action, just words. For me personally, saying "all sins are equal" gives me a slightly warmer feeling inside than when I say, "hate the sin, but not the sinner," which I don't think is even in the Bible.

We don't really believe that most times, though. Or rather, we only believe all sins are equal when our circle of friends is equal. It's easy to believe that when none of your friends has done anything with bigger consequences than something you've done. It's easy to believe all sins are equal when the worst sin you've heard confessed is that someone in your small group doesn't love their enemies enough. But it's a lot harder to believe that when you run into big, "gross" sins.

The idea of sin equality gets shaken when you meet a guy who cheated on his wife or stole hundreds of thousands of dollars from his company or used to work at a male strip club. It gets flipped upside down when a girl in your church admits she's had multiple abortions. Suddenly when you bump up against those things, the safe, comfortable belief that "all sins are equal" gets bruised a little. Like being relieved that someone behind you ran the red light even worse than you did, you think inside, "At least I haven't done *that*. Sure, I've made some mistakes, but I've never done *that*. That's a big sin right there."

And then you've got a little caste system going. You don't measure your sins against God's Word. You measure them against what other people are doing. You start to define holiness by a standard other than God's. The funny thing is, that approach usually works in your favor. If you look hard enough, you can usually find someone who's blowing it far worse than you, and knowing that you're not like them makes it a little easier to be like you.

The problem is that all sins are equal, even if the consequences aren't. The guy who goes to jail for his mistakes is certainly paying different consequences than the guy who downloaded some porn, but all sins are equal. And I think they're equal because God doesn't make the same distinctions that we do. His mind is not like ours. He's not up in heaven playing Galaga with Gideon, saying, "Oh no, Martin had an affair. Oh wait! It was just an emotional affair, not a physical affair. Phew! That was a close one."

I think all sins are equal because anything that distracts us from God's purpose for our lives has the same result: we're missing out on God's purpose for our lives. He's designed us for a special, perfect thing, and when we choose anything other than that, we miss it. The specifics of why we missed it probably matter less than we think. What we missed is what matters. God's big, crazy gift of love goes unclaimed for another hour ... another day ... another year. Whether you decided to ignore it because you were chasing money or girls or pie or a million other things isn't the point. You missed the gift, and that's what God cares about. You missed another day for him to let you know how much he loves you and how important you are.

That's why, even if we don't believe it sometimes, I think all sins are equal.

GUILT TRIPS

If God grades on a guilt system, then I want to be up front with you: my house in heaven is going to be sick. I don't know if we're still judging things by their proximity to "the hook," but if we are, you should consider my heaven house to be "off." There's going to be waterslides, everywhere. Not just in the pool, but between rooms. You want to get a Capri Sun from the kitchen? Hop on a waterslide. You want to go watch C. S. Lewis arm wrestle Aragorn from Lord of the Rings in the Ruckus Room? Hop on a waterslide.

That last thought didn't even make sense. What's a fictional character doing in heaven? Am I really going to call my living room the "Ruckus Room" because that's where the Ruckus happens and the floor is made of trampolines and the walls are made of blue cotton candy and to get in you have to open presents and watch old episodes of Seinfeld? Yes, that is exactly what I am going to do, especially if the amount of shame we inflict on ourselves has anything to do with how big our mansion is in heaven.

My greatest source of shame, the record I like to spin the most, is called, "The Ways Jon Lets God Down." Have you ever heard that one? It's got some jams on it, including:

1. Jon should know better by now but still makes the same mistakes.
2. Jon gets arrogant when something good happens and only comes to God when life is raining.
3. Jon makes God look horrible by telling everyone he's a Christian and then wrecking things he touches.
4. Jon wrestles with the simplest elements of faith and will never be a good enough Christian.

I could go on and on; it's an album I'm really familiar with, but lately it's getting harder to play it. Lately, as I've started to explore my shame with God, I've started to think that maybe God sees my shame and desire to beat myself into submission with guilt differently than I do. Maybe if I asked him what he thought, he'd say:

What if you struck yourself in the head with a chain every time you felt guilty or ashamed for letting me down? What if you physically punished yourself every time you were not perfect? What if the self abuse was physical and external, instead of mental and internal? Would the scars cry for help? Would the pain you were causing yourself seem cruel and unnecessary? Would your heart break if you watched that person? This is what I see when I watch you, Jonathan.

My son, my son, who told you that the crucifixion was not over?

Saying the word *crucifixion* is one of those Christian words that kind of make you look odd. You'll never hear a rapper at the Grammys or an athlete throwing out a verbal high five to God say, "Big shout-out to God. Thank you for the crucifixion of Christ."

I never realized that by beating myself up, I was putting on a parade of pain before the Lord as a way to enter his presence. And I never really thought about that hurting him. Not because he's disappointed, but because he loves me. Madly, passionately, unabashedly, he loves us.

TRYING HARDER

I'm not a big fan of exaggeration, which is why I don't casually make the following sentence:

"Chuck E. Cheese is the most terrifying place I've ever taken my oldest daughter."

It wasn't the man-sized rodent character that haunts the floor of this family fun center or the wooden balls they give toddlers to throw for skeeball, or even my fear of people who have single-letter middle names (I've got nothing but love for you, Samuel L. Jackson). It was the maze.

For starters, it's attached to the ceiling. So when your three-year-old wants to play in it they have to climb a series of ladders as if they are entering the terrordome. Then, once they're inside, they simply disappear. As a parent you pace the floor nervously, bumping into tables of people enjoying birthday cake, staring up at the ceiling trying to deduce which of the shadows in the thick, brightly colored plastic tubes is your kid. Occasionally you'll see her press her head and hands against a window in the maze similar to how an impassioned inmate would during their phone call with a loved one.

"Is she okay? Is she mouthing, 'Help, these tunnels are infested with eight-year-old boys'? Is she having a good time?" It's impossible to tell and there's no clear plan for her removal. Unless Chuck E. Cheese has some sort of vacuum system to suck kids out of the ceiling maze, you just have to hope your kid will eventually find the exit and crawl down to terra firma.

It wasn't always this way. I remember going to Chuck E.

Cheese as a child and loving the animatronic music show and the pizza. Best of all though was perhaps the ice cream bar. As a kid, having access to my own supply of jimmies or sprinkles was mind-blowing. Usually your parents were too distracted watching everyone else at your party, so you could pile on sprinkles into your bowl of ice cream until the bowl was 90 percent sprinkles, 10 percent ice cream.

Not everyone was able to handle the pressure though. I remember when I was in the second grade watching a fifth grader fall apart at the ice cream bar. The problem he faced was that the hot dog bar was right next to it. While I was waiting in line I watched him take a big bowl of pristine white soft serve vanilla ice cream and approach the first condiment dispenser. He pressed down hard and out came a serving of mustard.

It was all over his ice cream and he looked down at it with complete and utter devastation. I felt bad for him but out of nowhere a Chuck E. Cheese employee jumped in and said, "Here, that's okay. Here's a new bowl of ice cream. That's okay. Here you go; have some new ice cream."

I'll never forget that little boy's face as he looked up at the employee and down at his ruined bowl of ice cream. He was so ashamed at what he had done, so embarrassed that he had put mustard on it that he paused and then told the employee, "I'm fine. I'm fine. It's not a big deal. I'm fine." And then he started to stir the mustard into the ice cream.

He tried as hard as he could to mix that bright yellow mustard into the bright white vanilla ice cream. Finally it all became this pale emo-yellow-colored mush. He looked back up and then returned to his table, presumably to choke down his mustard ice cream.

I don't know about your life, but I've put a lot worse than mustard in my bowl of ice cream. I've got motor oil and D-batteries and a dead bird in there. And for most of my adult life, I thought that being a Christian just meant stirring harder. Maybe I had some different tools than people that weren't Christians, like reading my Bible or prayer, but ultimately it was up to me to try harder. To stir harder until I was a good enough Christian or a righteous enough Christian or a holy enough Christian.

But when I came to the end of me, when I finally saw how broken my bowl really was and realized that I could not fix me, with me, I learned a secret.

Jesus came for the sick.

Not the holy.

Not the righteous.

Not the perfect.

Not even the average.

He came for the sick.

He didn't come to take just the good people with him on a bus, and say it was okay if the sick folks like me clung to the side or rode on the roof. He came for us, the broken, the beaten, the severely messed up. Like me. Like you.

In Mark 2:17 Jesus says, "It is not the healthy who need a doctor, but the sick. I have not come to call the righteous, but sinners."

When I bumped into that truth, it changed the way I saw my ruined bowl of ice cream. It was no longer something I needed to stir and try to make perfect. It was no longer something I imagined Jesus and God being disgusted by. My wasted years and broken promises were no longer something I needed to hide.

My bowl was a lighthouse for a doctor that was looking for me, a neon sign that flashed, "Help, I'm over here! I need you! I need you!"

I don't know what's in your bowl, but I know that it's miserable to eat mustard ice cream and stirring as hard as we can is exhausting. So let's quit trying to be enough or make things work. Let's stop trying so hard.

Let's be sick. Let's be loved.

Which makes no sense. There's nothing else in life that works this way, where you can break something over and over and over again. And when you admit it, when you hold the pieces in your hand, you're met with the last thing you could ever think possible, love. That's ridiculous, but I think that's the gospel in four words.

Be sick. Be loved.

WRITING MULTIPLE VERSIONS OF THE SAME BOOK

By the time you finish reading this book, I will have written five more versions:

Stuff Christian Teens Like
Stuff Christian Parents Like
Stuff Christian Singles Like
Stuff Christian Ladies Like
Stuff Christian Red-Headed Uncles Like

You laugh, but the red-headed uncle market is pretty untapped and I've got a lot of ideas that apply directly to men that have red hair and nieces or nephews.

Plus, as I said in the introduction, I need lettuce for my shoe fetish and spinning off this book with a thousand different renditions is the best way to get that.

Wait a second. Did I really start and close this book with some lyrics from a Fergie song? I was hoping it would have been a Bible verse that tied the whole thing together, maybe something serious sounding from Job in the introduction and then something lighthearted from the book of Matthew in the last essay.

I'm so embarrassed. I don't have anything to say for myself except perhaps,

the end.

ACKNOWLEDGMENTS

First and foremost, I want to thank God and Jesus Christ. Not in a "rapper wins a Grammy holla' at God" kind of way but more in a "your love is so big and beautiful and ridiculous for me I can't fathom it" kind of way.

Jenny Acuff, without your encouragement, generosity, and constant wisdom this book never would have happened. You are hott with two t's. I love you. L.E. and McRae, my amazing daughters, you keep our house full of laughter and light. I love you. Mom and Dad, thank you for constantly showing me the joy of creativity and teaching me to laugh. You were doing this long before I was dad. Thanks for such a great example of what it means to be a man of God who can also laugh and throw a Frisbie. Will, Bennett, and Molly Acuff for turning the Acuff dinner table into some sort of Def Jam comedy hour. Will and Tiffany for giving me a home in Nashville. John and Laura Calbert, thank you for breaking every negative stereotype of what it means to be an in-law. You also bought me 1,000 SCL stickers for an event two people attended. Thank you for the optimism. Marci and Justin Saknini, thank you for getting a dog.

Andy Meisenheimer for amplifying every bit of this book with your own editing awesomeness. You are a great editor. Mrs. Harris, my third grade teacher at Doyon Elementary School in Ipswich, Massachusetts, who laminated a book of ridiculous poetry I wrote, forever sealing in my mind a love of writing and laminators. Dr. Jones, Dr. Clemmensen, and Dr. Shipley at Samford University. Billy Ivey, who is much funnier than me and needs to publish the Greyhound. Chip MacGregor, my fantastic literary agent. Brad Lomenick for showing me what it means to be a leader. Ryan Sweet. Mike Salisbury, Becky Philpott, Tom Dean, Angela Scheff, and the whole crew at Zondervan.

You guys made writing and publishing a book really fun. Mark Sheeres, your illustrations made everything funnier. Anne Jackson for going first. Beth Corbitt for agreeing to read the manuscript in exchange for a pound cake.

Brannon and Kendra Golden for reading the book before anyone else and teaching me the meaning of hospitality. Dana MacArthur. Jeff Johnson. Troy Haas. Bryan Allain, Tripp Crosby, and Tyler Stanton. Curtis Honeycutt, Nick the Geek, Hucklebuck, Katdish, Helen, Stacy from Louisville, Matt from the Church of No People, Marni, Karen Linton, Becky MIller, Dewde, and Donna. Pete Wilson. Matthew Paul Turner. Steven Pressfield and the beautifully written *The War of Art*. Anne Lamont and *Bird by Bird*. Joel Thomas. Mike Foster for stressing the importance of staying dangerous. John Saddington. Carlos Whittaker. Christian Lander, the founder of Stuff White People Like, which was the original inspiration for Stuff Christians Like. AutoTrader.com. Jason Boyett. Patty Youngblood. Kaye Cagle. Chris and Lori Windham. Dawn Nicole Baldwin. Mark Bennardo and Terrell Sanders. Abraham Piper. Nathan Beavers. Tim Challies. Boomama.net. Ben Arment. Joanna, the best SCL dictionary writer ever. Brian and Carrie Workman. Mike, Lynn, Wendy, and most importantly, the delightful Erin Maybury. Matt Waller. Whoever first called "fine" the Christian F-word because it wasn't me and that phrase is awesome. Brad Bretz. John Williams and the *Harry Potter* score, and Miles Davis' *Blue*, although those are particularly the same album. I don't know why I bothered to mention both except perhaps the hope that the coolness of the second one would offset what a huge dork I am. Chuck Allen, thank you for sharing your creativity and naming the chapter about quitting a prayer list. Josh Murphy for coming up with the dedication.

And all the readers of stuffchristianslike.net. Your kindness and overall hilarity is the reason this book got published. Thank you so much for going on this weird ride with me.

Anyone I forgot, I'm going to say what people who forget your prayer request say the world over—God remembers you.

WANT MORE
STUFF CHRISTIANS LIKE?

Visit stuffchristianslike.net

There are over 700 fresh essays and ideas just like the ones in this book. Plus, you can engage in a global conversation with readers from more than 200 countries.

Ideas include:

#606.–Finding creative things to say when someone dies.

#550.–Surviving church as a single.

#332.–That dude with the guitar at camp.

#325.–The superhero guide to famous pastors.

#304.–The sound guy/girl—In haiku form

#192.–Using "love on" as a verb.

#90.–The tankini.

#1.–Putting a God spin on popular secular ideas.

And many, many more.

If you've got an idea that belongs on the list of Stuff Christians Like, please let me know. Email me at jon@stuffchristians like.net or follow me on Twitter@prodigaljohn.

Thanks for reading.

See you online.

Razzle Dazzle.

—Jon

Share Your Thoughts

With the Author: Your comments will be forwarded to the author when you send them to *zauthor@zondervan.com*.

With Zondervan: Submit your review of this book by writing to *zreview@zondervan.com*.

Free Online Resources at

www.zondervan.com

Zondervan AuthorTracker: Be notified whenever your favorite authors publish new books, go on tour, or post an update about what's happening in their lives at www.zondervan.com/authortracker.

Daily Bible Verses and Devotions: Enrich your life with daily Bible verses or devotions that help you start every morning focused on God. Visit www.zondervan.com/newsletters.

Free Email Publications: Sign up for newsletters on Christian living, academic resources, church ministry, fiction, children's resources, and more. Visit www.zondervan.com/newsletters.

Zondervan Bible Search: Find and compare Bible passages in a variety of translations at www.zondervanbiblesearch.com.

Other Benefits: Register yourself to receive online benefits like coupons and special offers, or to participate in research.

ZONDERVAN®

ZONDERVAN.com/
AUTHORTRACKER
follow your favorite authors